148°

Camera in the Interior: 1858

H. L. HIME, PHOTOGRAPHER

THE ASSINIBOINE AND SASKATCHEWAN EXPLORING EXPEDITION

Richard J. Huyda

THE COACH HOUSE PRESS, TORONTO

To my father and mother

The photograph, however, cannot deceive; in nothing can it extenuate; there is no power in this marvellous machine either to add or to take from: we know that what we see must be TRUE. So guided, therefore, we can travel over all countries of the world, without moving a yard from our own firesides. Fortunately there are those who, from love of wandering, or of Art, or of gain, will incur any amount of fatigue and danger, and bring to us enjoyment and knowledge, without demanding from us either labour or risk; giving in an hour the information that has been gained by years of toil and peril. All honour to the men who are thus our ministers!

The Art Journal 1860, p.221

Acknowledgements

I wish to express my gratitude to Dr W.I. Smith, Dominion Archivist, and to the senior management of the Public Archives of Canada for allowing me to use the research notes, the original Hime Photographs and various collections of the Public Archives. I am also grateful to John Bovey, Provincial Archivist of Manitoba, for access to the Hime Notebook; to Edith Firth of the Toronto Public Library for the use of the Hime photograph of Ojibways at Fort Frances; and to the Reverend Campbell Russell of the Church of St Stephen-in-the-Fields, Toronto, for access to the parish registers.

To Dr W.L. Morton and Ralph Greenhill I owe a two-fold debt. I was fortunate in having Dr Morton as teacher and advisor and Ralph Greenhill's pioneer work on early photography in Canada as a guide and inspiration. Moreover, both men read my manuscript and offered invaluable criticism and encouragement.

I am particularly indebted to my editor Linda Davey who spent many an hour redeeming my literary sins.

To my colleagues and staff at the Public Archives of Canada I extend heartfelt appreciation for their advice, continuing encouragement and assistance. My thanks are also due to Elizabeth Blight and her colleagues at the Manitoba Archives; to Lionel Dorge of La Societé de St Boniface; and to the helpful staffs of the Notman Photographic Archives, the Toronto City Archives, and the Toronto Public Library. If there are others whom I have failed to mention I extend my thanks and apologies here.

I would be remiss if I did not acknowledge the dedicated work of Stan Bevington and his staff at the Coach House Press. Their skills, enthusiasm and quest for quality have created this book.

Finally, to my wife Elaine and to my children I offer this book as small reward for their tolerance and love.

Richard J. Huyda

Contents

Part I
A Portfolio of H. L. Hime Photographs

The Photographs

1 Ojibways at Fort Frances, May 24, 1858.

2 Ojibway Encampment near the Falls of the Rainy River, May 24, 1858.

3 Encampment on the Red River. Members of the Assiniboine and Saskatchewan Exploring Expedition, June 1, 1858.

4 Making a portage. Voyageurs and canoemen of the Expedition, June 2, 1858.

5 Valley of the Souris, July 3, 1858.

6 Encampment – Little Souris, July 3, 1858.

7 Fort Ellice – Beaver Creek, July 11, 1858.

8 Valley of the Calling River (Qu'Appelle Valley), July 18, 1858.

9 View of a valley (probably Qu'Appelle Valley), July 18, 1858.

10 Qu'Appelle Lakes, July 18, 1858.

11 Fort Pelly, July 27–August 3, 1858.

12 Fort Pelly, July 27–August 3, 1858.

13 View of Red River, from the Stone Fort, September–October, 1858.

14 View of Red River, from St Andrew's Church, four miles above the Stone Fort, September–October, 1858.

15 Red River; Middle Settlement, eight miles below Fort Garry, September–October, 1858.

16 Freighter's Boat on the banks of Red River, seven miles below Fort Garry, (the white patch in the foreground is snow), September– October, 1858.

17 Bishop's Court (the residence of the Bishop of Rupert's Land) on the banks of Red River, September–October, 1858.

18 Cathedral of St Boniface (Roman Catholic) and Nunnery, on the banks of Red River, opposite Fort Garry, September–October, 1858.

19 St John's Church, two miles below Fort Garry (Church of England), September–October, 1858.

36 John McKay; a Plain-Cree half-breed, September–October, 1858.

37 Letitia: a Plain-Cree half-breed, September–October, 1858.

38 Jane L'Adamar (sometimes captioned 'Susan: a Swampy-Cree half-breed).

39 Wigwam: an Ojibway half-breed, Lake Superior, September–October, 1858.

40 An Ojibway Squaw with Papoose, September–October, 1858.

41 A Blackfoot Warrior's Robe, containing a history of his wars, and buffalo hunts, and showing the number of scalps he has taken from his enemies, September–October, 1858.

42 Tents on the prairie, September–October, 1858.

43 Red River Freighter's boat, September–October, 1858.

44 The Prairie looking west, September–October, 1858.

45 Residence of Chief Factor (the late Mr Bird), September–October, 1858.

46 Quarters of the Expedition at Red River, September–October, 1858.

47 Stone Fort, Lower Fort Garry, September–October, 1858.

48 Dog Carioles; part of the Expedition returning to Crow Wing, by the winter road, Tuesday, November 30, 1858.

49 Fossil resting on book entitled *Natural History of New York*, September–November, 1858.
See Part Two, Appendix II for an inventory of known Hime photographs in Canadian repositories.

2 Ojibway Encampment near the Falls of the Rainy River, May 24, 1858.

1 Ojibways at Fort Frances, May 24, 1858.

3   Encampment on the Red River. Members of the Assiniboine and Saskatchewan Exploring Expedition, June 1, 1858.

4   Making a portage. Voyageurs and canoemen of the Expedition, June 2, 1858.

5 Valley of the Souris, July 3, 1858.

6   Encampment – Little Souris, July 3, 1858.

7   Fort Ellice – Beaver Creek, July 11, 1858.

8 Valley of the Calling River (Qu'Appelle Valley), July 18, 1858.

9   View of a valley (probably Qu'Appelle Valley), July 18, 1858.

10 Qu'Appelle Lakes, July 18, 1858.

11 Fort Pelly, July 27–August 3, 1858.

12 Fort Pelly, July 27–August 3, 1858.

13 View of Red River, from the Stone Fort, September–October, 1858.

14 View of Red River, from St Andrew's Church, four miles above the Stone Fort, September–October, 1858.

15 Red River; Middle Settlement, eight miles below Fort Garry, September–October, 1858.

16 Freighter's Boat on the banks of Red River, seven miles below Fort Garry, (the white patch in the foreground is snow), September– October, 1858.

17 Bishop's Court (the residence of the Bishop of Rupert's Land) on the banks of Red River, September–October, 1858.

18 Cathedral of St Boniface (Roman Catholic) and Nunnery, on the banks of Red River, opposite Fort Garry, September–October, 1858.

19 St John's Church, two miles below Fort Garry (Church of England), September–October, 1858.

20 Presbyterian Church and Parsonage, seven miles below Fort Garry, September–October, 1858.

21 St Paul's Church, Parsonage, and School House, eight and a half miles below Fort Garry (Church of England), September – October, 1858.

22 St Andrew's Church (Rapids Church), sixteen miles below Fort Garry (Church of England),
September–October, 1858.

23 St Andrew's Parsonage, September–October, 1858.

24 Residence of Mr Bannatyne, a general trader near Fort Garry, September–October, 1858.

25 Mr McDermot's Store, near Fort Garry. One of the first houses erected at Red River, September–October, 1858.

26 Farm-houses and windmills, Middle Settlement. A vast expanse of level prairie lying to the west in the rear of the dwellings, September–October, 1858.

27 Mr Hingster's (Inkster) house and farm buildings, September– October, 1858.

28 Ojibway tents on the banks of Red River, near the Middle Settlement, September–October, 1858.

29 Birch-bark tents, west bank of Red River, Middle Settlement, September–October, 1858.

30 Indian graves, covered with split sticks. An enemy's scalp is usually suspended from the thin poles overhanging the grave, September–October, 1858.

31 Indian graves, covered with birch bark (the patch of white in the foreground is snow), September–October, 1858.

32 The Prairie, on the banks of Red River, looking south, September–October, 1858.

33 Fort Garry; at the confluence of Red River and the Assiniboine, September–October, 1858.

34 Hon. Hudson's Bay Company's Officers' quarters: Lower or Stone Fort, September–October, 1858.

35 Fur Store: interior of Lower or Stone Fort, September–October, 1858.

36 John McKay; a Plain-Cree half-breed, September–October, 1858.

37 Letitia: a Plain-Cree half-breed, September–October, 1858.

38 Jane L'Adamar (sometimes captioned 'Susan: a Swampy-Cree half-breed).

39 Wigwam: an Ojibway half-breed, Lake Superior, September–October, 1858.

40 An Ojibway Squaw with Papoose, September–October, 1858.

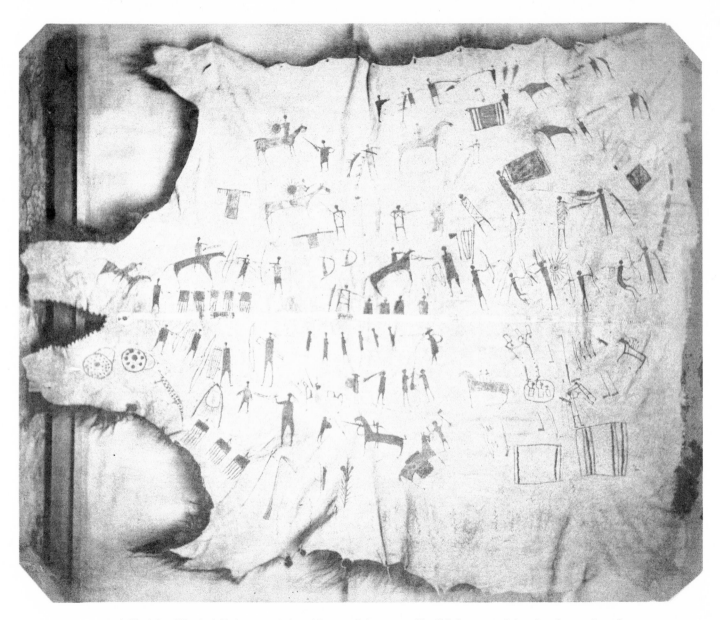

41 A Blackfoot Warrior's Robe, containing a history of his wars, and buffalo hunts, and showing the number of scalps he has taken from his enemies, September–October, 1858.

42 Tents on the prairie, September–October, 1858.

43 Red River Freighter's boat, September–October, 1858.

44 The Prairie looking west, September–October, 1858.

45 Residence of Chief Factor (the late Mr Bird), September–October, 1858.

46 Quarters of the Expedition at Red River, September–October, 1858.

47 Stone Fort, Lower Fort Garry, September–October, 1858.

48 Dog Carioles; part of the Expedition returning to Crow Wing, by the winter road, Tuesday, November 30, 1858.

49 Fossil resting on book entitled *Natural History of New York*, September–November, 1858.

Part II
H. L. Hime and the Assiniboine and
Saskatchewan Exploring Expedition

CHAPTER I

Background

In British North America there were several factors which stimulated the Imperial and Canadian Governments to sponsor exploring expeditions into the Western Interior during the 1850s. There was renewed imperial concern for more secure links with its far western colony in British Columbia where gold had been discovered and the Pacific Coast was of growing importance to British oriental trade interests. In the interior the small communities along the Red River had been expanding. It was undesirable that they continue to remain isolated and exposed to American Western expansion.

Moreover, the monopoly of the Hudson's Bay Company to exclusive trade in the vast regions of the interior would expire in 1859. The Company desired an extension of its monopoly, but the Canadian Government had indicated to Britain that it was extremely interested in extending its jurisdiction westward from the Great Lakes. Settlement of the interior and a communication link between all the British possessions in North America seemed desirable imperial goals, but their feasibility was uncertain without more thorough investigation of the area.

In 1857 two exploratory expeditions were sent into the western interior. These expeditions were to concentrate on an accurate objective description of the geography, to define and identify the topography and resources of the area, to study the geology, climate, vegetation and native life, assess the agricultural and settlement potential and report on the possibilities of a permanent communication route linking all the British North American colonies. The observations of the expeditions were to be embodied in official written reports and in an accurate series of maps.

To undertake these tasks the British Government, on the advice of the Royal Geographical Society, sent out a combined military and civilian expedition under the direction of Captain John Palliser and Dr James Hector. The Palliser Expedition as it was later called, spent three years in its investigation of the area between Lake Superior and the Rockies. In 1860 the official reports of Palliser's Expedition were issued by the British Parliament.

The Canadian Government at the same time commissioned its first exploratory expedition. Its primary objective was

to make a thorough examination of the tract of country between Lake Superior and the Red River. By which may be determined the best route for opening a facile communication through British Territory, from that lake to the Red River Settlements, and ultimately to the great tracts of cultivable land beyond them. [1]

This expedition was comprised strictly of civilians. It was under the command of George

1 Canada: Legislative Assembly, *Report on the Exploration of the Country Between Lake Superior and the Red River Settlement.* (Toronto, 1858), p.5.

3

Gladman and was divided into three separate parties. One was led by Simon J. Dawson, a surveyor and engineer, whose task was to secure information on the topography and routes from Lake Superior to Red River. The second was led by Professor Henry Youle Hind, geologist and naturalist at Trinity College, Toronto. He was to describe the main geological features of the country and whatever pertained to its natural history. The third party was led by W.H. Napier, engineer. This first Canadian expedition arrived at Fort William on July 31, 1857 and working until September gradually approached the Red River Settlements. After a further month's work at the Settlements Hind returned to Toronto, while Dawson and Napier wintered at Red River.

CHAPTER II

Preparations for the 1858 expedition

On the basis of preliminary reports from the first expedition the Canadian Government decided to continue the geographical investigations the following year with two divisions extending their activities from the Red River to the South Saskatchewan River. Simon Dawson was placed in charge of one division. After a general reconnaissance through Lakes Winnipeg, Manitoba, and Winnipegosis to the Saskatchewan River at Cedar Lake and returning over the Manitoba Escarpment through the Swan River and Assiniboine valleys, he was to resume his task of surveying the area between Red River and Lake Superior. Henry Youle Hind was to direct the second division on a topographical and geological expedition west of Red River. It is this latter expedtition with which we are basically concerned.

General instructions from the Provincial Secretary, T.J.J. Loranger were given verbally to Hind during the first week of April, 1858 and confirmed in writing on April 14. Hind's estimate of probable expenditures was approved and he was asked to organize his party, providing a list of the names of all members of the expedition and stating their rates of pay and dates of commencement. The expedition was then to depart as soon as possible.

More specific instructions for the guidance of the expedition were issued on April 27. The region to be explored was

that lying to the west of Lake Winnipeg and Red River, and embraced (or nearly so) between the rivers Saskatchewan and Assiniboine, as far west as 'South Branch House' on the former river, which latter place will be the most westerly point. [2]

The expedition was to procure information respecting the geology, natural history, topography and meteorology of the region. Specific observations were to be made of the rivers, the character of timber, soil, weather and agricultural potential. Also, a map on a scale of two miles to one inch was to be constructed and a collection made of any objects which would illustrate the natural history of the country. Hind was to be held responsible for the conduct, diligence and fidelity of the party. Finally, to identify the expedition for the present year it was to be designated as the 'Assiniboine and Saskatchewan Exploring Expedition'.

In the instructions there was no specific requirement for photographic documentation. Indeed, the reasoning behind the decision to include a photographer is nowhere officially recorded. The Canadian Government had not yet recognized the potential of photography for its work. The only recorded official use of photography prior to 1858 was in 1857 when the Provincial Secretary issued payment to a Hamilton photographer for a series of views of the Great Desjardins Canal Railway Disaster. However, it had been

2 Hind, Henry Youle: *North-West Territory Reports of Progress; Together with a Preliminary and General Report on the Assiniboine and Saskatchewan Exploring Expedition, Made Under Instructions From the Provincial Secretary, Canada*. (Toronto, John Lovell, 1859) p. 2.

traditional practice to include in exploratory expeditions individuals possessing some artistic ability whose sketches might be used to illustrate the official reports of the expeditions. The 1857 Canadian Expedition had two artists of note: John Fleming and William Napier. Moreover, other Governments had in the past few years been employing photographers in their official expeditions. Two daguerreotypists had accompanied Commodore Perry on his official expedition for the u.s. to Japan in 1852. The u.s. survey party into the West in 1853 employed a photographer. Leading explorers of the day also advocated using photography extensively on expeditions.

In addition, photography was becoming more and more an acceptable part of life in urban Canada. Its potential to record with faithfulness was undoubtedly brought to the attention of many government officials who had themselves sat before a camera or had seen the views of such photographers as McLaughlin of Quebec, Notman of Montreal, or Palmer of Toronto. Thus, by 1858, Canadian Government officials were probably willing to accept without objection a reasonable expenditure for photography should this be suggested as a requirement for an exploratory expedition.

The initial decision to make use of photography on the 1858 expedition was probably Hind's personal action. He felt that photography could provide a most accurate record of places and things, and that its nature was such that any number of copies could be taken to illustrate a narrative of the expedition. He may have initially intended to take the photographs himself for his estimates of April 6 list under 'Instruments for Mr Hind' a requirement for complete photographic apparatus costing $200.00. But as he had encountered a man who combined the talents of photographer and surveyor he reconsidered his estimates, stroking out a previous entry for an 'Assistant to Mr Hind' and writing in pencil the word 'photographer' opposite the sum of $640.00.

These estimates of April 6 were laid before the Governor-General in Council and approved without objection that same week. On April 10 Hind informed the Provincial Secretary that he had completed the selection of personnel for the expedition. Along with himself as geologist he named James Dickinson as surveyor and John Fleming as assistant and draughtsman. Both of these men had been on the 1857 expedition. He also named a Mr Hime as photographer.

This Mr Hime, the photographer, was Humphrey Lloyd Hime, twenty-four year old junior partner of the firm of Armstrong, Beere and Hime, Civil Engineers, Draughtsmen and Photographists, 35 King Street East, Toronto, C.W. Born in Moy, Co. Armagh, Ireland on September 17, 1833 Hime had crossed to England at the age of fifteen to obtain a business education and learn textile manufacturing. In 1854 he came to Canada. Little is known of Hime's first year in Canada although it is likely that he worked

6

with surveying crews in Canada West, probably on the islands of Georgian Bay and Lake Simcoe. By September 25, 1855 he was employed as first chainman on a survey party under the direction of W.H. Napier. Napier's party was then working in the Bruce Peninsula surveying the Indian Reserve northwest of Owen Sound and Sangeen. Hime stayed with the party until January 10, 1856.

Shortly thereafter Hime joined William Armstrong and Daniel Beere in their Toronto firm. Napier, who was an accomplished artist as well as surveyor might have recommended Hime to Armstrong, who also was an artist and surveyor. Armstrong and Beere were impressed with their new colleague. By January of 1857 they accepted Hime as a junior partner and the firm was renamed Armstrong, Beere and Hime. [3] The association proved a fortunate one for Hime. Through his partners he was able both to enlarge his knowledge of surveying and perhaps, more importantly, to learn photography. Both Armstrong and Beere were experienced photographers. The firm had gained a reputation for excellence in its photographic work. At the Twelfth Annual Exhibition of the Provincial Agricultural Association held in Brantford in 1857 the firm was awarded first and second prize for the 'best collection of photographs (uncolourd)' and second prize for the best coloured photographs.

By 1858 Hime was a talented and ambitious young man who combined a sound knowledge and experience in surveying with a mastery of the art of photography. Henry Youle Hind recognized that Hime could be a useful member of his staff. Their meeting was probably not coincidental, but arranged through a mutual acquaintance, perhaps W.H. Napier or William Armstrong. As has been noted previously, Hime was on Napier's staff on the Bruce Peninsula Survey of 1855-56. The following year Napier was the engineer on the Red River Expedition and had travelled west to Fort Frances with Hind. Hind and William Armstrong, both members of the Canadian Institute, were probably acquainted with each other and might have discussed young Hime's qualifications for the expedition.

Hind and Hime may have held some preliminary discussions about the 1858 expedition prior to April 6. If this was the case it might account for Hind's deletion of the term 'Assistant to Mr. Hind' and his substitution of the term 'Photographer' in his estimates of that date. Certainly he and Hime had made final arrangements by April 10, for Hind wrote to the Provincial Secretary on that date and listed Hime as Photographer to be paid at the rate of £20 per month. He concluded this letter by stating that

Mr. Hime is a practical photographer of the service of Armstrong, Hime and Beere, Toronto. In addition to the qualification of being an excellent photographer, he is also a practical surveyor, and

3 The firm of Armstrong, Beere & Hime seems to have existed as early as December, 1856. A watercolour by Armstrong in the Sigmund Samuel Collection of the Royal Ontario Museum bears an execution date of December, 1856 with Armstrong's signature, and in the lower left corner the embossed stamp of the firm. However, an advertisement in the January 2, 1857 issue of *The Globe* refers to the firm of Armstrong and Beere, but the January 26, 1857 issue lists the firm of Armstrong, Beere & Hime with a date at the bottom of the advertisement as January 20, 1857.

it is understood that when his services are not required for the practice of his particular department, he is to assist in the Surveying operations. Mr. Hime will furnish a series of Collodion Negatives for the full illustration of all objects of interest susceptible of photographic delineation, from which any number of copies can be taken to illustrate a narrative of the Expedition and a report on its results. [4]

Hime was officially offered the position on April 12. He replied on April 13, agreeing to the terms of employment. He would occupy the position of Photographer at a salary of 20a month, plus expenses. In return, his work was to belong exclusively to the Canadian Government and he was 'to make himself useful in every way he could'. [5] On April 14, Hime was officially taken on staff.

The hiring of professional staff was only one aspect of the many preparations to be made that April. Hind had also to arrange for the purchase of provisions, equipment, instruments, canoes and canoemen. Many of the supplies were available in Toronto. A.M. Smith and the firm of Boyd and Arthur served as grocery provisioners while the firm of Hearn & Potter supplied surveying and mathematical instruments. But not everything was obtainable in Toronto.

On April 9 Hind informed the Provincial Secretary that he intended to travel to Montreal and Lachine on the following Tuesday 'for the purpose of securing the services of Iroquois Indians, purchasing canoes, camp equipage, probably photographic Apparatus, and some necessary articles not to be found in Toronto...'. [6] By Thursday, April 16 he was in Lachine visiting Sir George Simpson, Governor of the Hudson Bay Company, and on Friday he made arrangements with fourteen Iroquois at Caughnawagna to serve as canoemen to Red River. Whether Hind purchased the photographic apparatus in Montreal or acquired it in Toronto is unknown. Perhaps he arranged to secure it from the firm of Armstrong, Beere & Hime. Whatever the case, on April 23 Hind reported that all arrangements for the expedition were completed.

Hind was aware of the Victorian interest in colonial explorations and did not want to miss any opportunity of ensuring that his expedition would receive exposure in the press. A week before the Expedition was to depart he wrote to the Provincial Secretary seeking permission

to endeavour to make arrangements with Mr. McKay, the Editor in Chief of the Illustrated London News, and now in this city, to have published in the London Illustrated News, a series of sketches of the forts belonging to the Hon. Hudson's Bay Co., of Indians and of Scenery, either drawn by hand or taken by photograph during the proposed exploration of the vallies of the Assiniboine and Saskatchewan under my charge. [7]

4 Public Archives of Canada (PAC), Record Group (RG) 5, C I, Vol. 578–579, No. 761.

5 PAC, RG 5, C I, Vol. 707, 1862, No. 557, H.L. Hime to H.Y. Hind, Toronto, April 13, 1858.

6 PAC, RG 5, C I, Vol. 555, 1858, No. 733.

7 PAC, RG 5, C I, Vol. 578–579, 1858, No. 907, H.Y. Hind to the Provincial Secretary, Toronto, April 23, 1858.

Each sketch and photograph was to be accompanied by a brief description and sent to the Provincial Secretary for inspection and approval before transmission to London. Hind's suggestions were accepted and arrangements were subsequently made with the *Illustrated London News*.

PHOTOGRAPHS
Of all descriptions,
Executed in the best style.
Plans & Drawings
Of every description,
COPIED OR DESIGNED.
DOCUMENTS,
Requiring accurate copies,
Photographed.
Photographs furnished to Lithographers.

TERMS--CASH.

55 KING STREET EAST,

Toronto, May 4th 1859

H. Y. Hind on a/c of Assiniboine & Saskatchewan Exploring Expedition

To Armstrong, Beere & Hime, Dr.

March			$	C
	To D. Beere assisting Hime one month at $80.00		80	00

CHAPTER III

The expedition underway

to Red River

April–June

8 The chronological and logistical information concerning the movements of the Expedition from April until November of 1858 are taken mainly from Hind, H.Y., *Narrative of the Canadian Red River Exploring Expedition of 1857 and of the Assiniboine and Saskatchewan Exploring Expedition of 1858*, two volumes (London, Longman, Green, Longman and Roberts, 1860) and from Hind, H.Y., *North-West Territory Reports of Progress; Together with a Preliminary and General Report on the Assiniboine and Saskatchewan Exploring Expedition, Made Under Instructions From the Provincial Secretary, Canada*, (Toronto, John Lovell, 1859).

Hind, his staff and Iroquois voyageurs left Toronto at one o'clock on April 29. Travelling on the Great Western Railway they arrived at Detroit the following day and boarded the steamer *Illinois* for the journey up the Lakes. On May 2 the steamer stopped at Sault Ste Marie to take on further supplies and then proceeded across Lake Superior. The steamer brought the party to Grand Portage on May 5 since the expedition was to travel to Red River by way of the old North West Company Pigeon River canoe route rather than by the more frequented Fort William-Kaministiquia route. [8]

The next five days were spent conveying canoes and six thousand pounds of baggage across the eight mile portage. On May 10 or 11 the expedition began the arduous canoe journey along the rivers and lakes to Red River. The journey of twenty-eight days to Red River was a prelude to the coming months of life in the interior. The party was underway before dawn each morning. They travelled steadily until dusk with few breaks in spite of frequently inclement weather. Hime must have realized during these first days that there would be no time in a normal day's travel to set up his photographic equipment. Only the infrequent long rest periods or enforced delays would afford him this opportunity. Even then so much would depend upon the weather and the amount of other work to be done.

The first full day's halt came at Fort Frances on May 24. Here the expedition stopped to repair the canoes, unload the supplies for Dawson's party, to rest, and to celebrate Her Majesty's Birthday. This was Hime's first opportunity to unpack his photographic equipment. As might be expected he sought to photograph the fort and the local native inhabitants.

Two photographs are definitely known to have been taken. He succeeded in obtaining a view of a group of Ojibway indians near the palisades of the Fort and another of an Ojibway group at their encampment near the Falls of the Rainy River. An original print of the group near the palisades has survived, but the only record of the other photo is a copy engraving which later appeared in the *Illustrated London News*. It is evident from these two records that Hime possessed a mastery of composition although he had not yet mastered the intricacies of his equipment. There is evidence of lack of clarity in focus and flaws due possibly to improper processing. This could be expected as Hime was working with new apparatus and under relatively unfamiliar conditions – indeed, under far different conditions from the organized and well supplied studio of a city establishment.

Hime probably realized that his first attempts would be mainly experimental and any faults or problems would be corrected only with experience. But he probably was not prepared for one crucial variant in wilderness photography: the suspicion and fears of the indian peoples. Unlike the citizens who had complacently posed before his camera in Toronto the indians of Fort Frances were not all willing subjects.

When an attempt was made to take a photograph of the interior of one of the lodges, several squaws, who were seated with their children around the fires, instantly rose, and, driving the children before them, hastened off to the neighbouring forest, and no arguments or presents could induce them to remain. They said that 'the white wanted to take their pictures and send them far away to the great chief of the white men, who would make evil medicine over them, and when the pictures were sent back the Indians who were drawn would all perish. They knew this was the way the white man wanted to get rid of the Indians and take their land'. Many of the men had this impression, and carefully moved out of reach of the camera.[9]

But despite the mixed success of these first attempts Hime would learn to adapt the intricacies of collodion wet-plate photography to the wilderness environment.

When Hime left Toronto the previous month he took with him a complete complement of photographic apparatus. His camera had a two inch portrait and a two inch landscape lens with a field of f x 7¼. The rest of his supplies, including chemicals, containers, etc., conformed exactly to the requirements listed in Hardwich's *Manual of Photographic Chemistry*,[10] a copy of which he had packed with his equipment. This manual was to serve him, as it did most of the photographers of the day, as a basic guide, offering complete instructions on the practice of wet-plate photography.[11]

In the final stages of the trip to the Red River Settlements Hime again had an opportunity to use his camera. The expedition had made a rapid voyage from Rainy Lake. The remaining trip up the Red River would be less taxing on the men. Hind did not press the guide. Rest periods were probably longer and more leisurely with sufficient time to unpack and set up the photographic equipment.

The party camped off the mouth of the Red River on June 1. It was probably during this encampment that Hime photographed the officers of the expedition relaxing in front of their upturned canoe. The following day, during the noon-day meal he again set up his camera. The Iroquois voyageurs had almost completed their tasks as far as the expedition was concerned. A documentary photograph of the men in action was in order and he captured for posterity the canoemen in a pose so characteristic and so common to those men who had gone through the same motions so many times before during the past twenty-eight days.

These photographs of the expedition party have survived. They are of good technical quality. There is good composition, good use of light, and adequate processing. As documentary evidence they are invaluable. They record not just portraits of the participants, but reflect some of the rigours of their environment and that sense of adventure and freedom that motivated them to move on into the new interior.

9 *The Illustrated London News*, No. 941, Vol. XXXIII, October 16, 1858, pp. 366–367.
10 Hardwich, Thomas, Frederick, *A Manual of Photographic Chemistry Including the Practice of the Collodion Process* (London: John Churchill, 1859) Fifth Edition, pp. 263–264. Hime probably used either the second Edition published in New York by Humphrey in 1856 or a third edition published probably in New York in 1857.
11 See Appendix 1, page 30.

CHAPTER IV

The expedition at Red River

June 2–14

The expedition reached the Red River Settlements on the afternoon of June 2. Leaving supplies intended for Mr Dawson at the Middle Settlement Hind immediately began to organize a party to explore the country west along the Assiniboine to the South Saskatchewan. The preparations proved to be difficult. It was to take eleven days to obtain the necessary supplies and able-bodied men. Hind felt that he would need a strong party because of 'the distrust and even dread with which the Sioux Indians are regarded by the Red River Hunters … '.[12] But as he indicated in his report

In consequence … of the failure of last year's autumn buffalo hunt, and the ravages of the grasshoppers at Prairie Portage, and elsewhere in the Settlements, most of the able-bodied men fit for the exigencies of a journey into the Indian Country, had left the settlements a few days before my arrival, … it was with some difficulty that I could procure eight men and the necessary provisions for a three months journey …'.[13]

While making these preparations Hind wrote a preliminary report on the expedition. He forwarded this with Dickinson's Pigeon River report, maps and several photographs for the *Illustrated London News* to the Provincial Secretary in Toronto via the United States. These arrived in the Provincial Secretary's office on July 6. The photographs undoubtedly included the view of the Ojibway encampment at Fort Frances and the group view of the voyageurs encamped on the Red River, both of which later appeared in the October 16 issue of the *Illustrated London News*.

Hime, it appears, did not take any photographs during this initial stay at Red River. He may have been busy with the preparations for the expedition into the interior.

CHAPTER V

The expedition in the field

June 14–September 4

The party assembled at its temporary quarters in the Settlement on the morning of June 14 and loaded the five Red River carts and one wagon with two canoes, camp equipment, instruments and provisions. At noon the start was made. The train proceeded to Fort Garry some eight miles away and took on a supply of flour and pemmican. Then, camping about a half mile from the Fort they took inventory of their baggage and laid out the basic arrangements and regulations for the journey.

The party consisted initially of fourteen individuals. Along with Hind, Fleming, Dickinson, and Hime were six Cree half-breeds, one Red River native, a Blackfoot half-breed, Ojibway half-breed and one French Canadian. Later an old hunter of Cree origin was to be hired. In addition to the equipment already mentioned were fifteen horses and provisions consisting of

... One thousand pounds of flour, four hundred pounds of pemmican, one thousand rations of Crimean vegetables, a sheep, three hams, and tea for three months, with a few luxuries, such as pickles, chocolate, a gallon of port wine and one gallon of brandy. [14]

These supplies were to be supplemented later by the purchase of an additional Red River cart and an ox for food in case the buffalo were scarce.

On the morning of June 15 the journey into the interior began. The party stopped at St James' Church and split into two divisions. Hime and Fleming proceeded with the carts and wagon to Lane's Post and then to Prairie Portage which they reached by 1 pm on June 17. Here they awaited the afternoon arrival of Hind and Dickinson's party. The following day was spent repairing carts and making preparations to enter the Sioux country. It was here that the thunderstorms which were to plague the expedition for seventeen of the next twenty-three days began, augmenting the difficulties of the journey and, undoubtedly, limiting Hime's opportunity to take photographs.

On the morning of June 19 the whole party set out from Prairie Portage for the valley of the Little Souris. Along the way they encountered the first of many hordes of grasshoppers. The confluence of the Little Souris and the Assiniboine was reached on the afternoon of the 24th. The party then proceeded cautiously up the Little Souris, alert at all times for signs of the Sioux. Countless species of small game were observed, but there was no sign of buffalo. The absence of the spring herds was attributed to the fact that in the autumn of 1857 the whole prairie from the Red to the South Saskatchewan Rivers had been on fire: 'a vast conflagration extending for one thousand miles in length and several hundreds in breadth'. [15]

12 Hind, North-West Territory Reports ..., *op. cit.*; p.7.
13 *Loc. Cit.*
14 Hind, North-West Territory Reports ..., *op. cit.*; p.39.
15 *Ibid*, p.42.

On July 2 the expedition camped on the banks of Red Deer's Head River near its confluence with the Little Souris some two miles from the International Boundary. The expedition remained encamped until the late afternoon of July 3 to make observations as well as to repair the carts and travelling gear. During the rest period a detachment made a reconnaissance of the Red Deer's Head River to its mouth within a few yards of the 49th parallel. Hime accompanied the detachment and, while the other members made a further excursion to the Souris Lakes within U.S. territory in the hopes of finding buffalo, he set up his camera and took a photograph of the Little Souris Valley, the first photograph of the official part of the expedition. The reconnaissance party returned to camp in the afternoon and the whole expedition resumed its journey and camped some twelve miles away. That same day Hime took another photograph – that entitled 'Encampment Little Souris' – showing the five Red River carts, tents and some of the men. In the evening 'some hostile Sioux in ambuscade in the vicinity of the encampment, attempted to stampede the hobbled horses', but with no success. [16]

The following morning, July 4, the expedition headed nearly due north to cross the Great Prairie, heading for Fort Ellice near the confluence of the Qu'Appelle and Assiniboine rivers. The first day's journey towards Fort Ellice proved slow going as the horses were fatigued by the excessive heat. Only fourteen miles were made that day. However, the next five days of the journey were made at a fairly steady pace as the party was crossing relatively undulating prairie terrain, generally treeless and arid. Brief stops were made for meals, to take observations, ford streams, skin buffalo, or hunt for fossils. There was little time for photography. Moreover, there were thunderstorms almost daily and the grasshoppers continued to plague the expedition.

Of these insects Hind made countless references, speaking of their vast numbers and devasting ability to eat up the prairie grass, provisions, clothing and leather goods. At one point he wrote

Everywhere we find grasshoppers … innumerable hosts of grasshoppers were flying northward in the direction of the wind. At times they would cast a shadow over the prairie, and for several hours one day, the sky from the horizon, to an altitude of thirty degrees, acquired an indescribably brilliant and white tint, and seemed fairly luminous as the semi-transparent wings of countless millions of grasshoppers towards the north and north east, reflected the light of the sun. [17]

Fort Ellice was reached early on the morning of July 10. Fording the Beaver River the expedition camped on its banks within a half mile of the fort. They remained at this

16 Hind, North-West Territory Reports …, op. cit.; p. 45.
17 Ibid, p. 8.
18 Ibid, p. 138.
19 Hind, Narrative of the Canadian Red River …., op. cit., Vol. 1, p. 327.
20 Hind, North-West Territory Reports …, op. cit., p. 48.

encampment from the 10th until 4-5 pm on the 12th. The men rested, visited hunters from the Fort, took on a supply of pemmican, made various observations, and did some brief reconnoitering. During this time there were more thunderstorms; not a day passing without lightning, thunder and violent rain of a half an hour's duration. Fortunately, on Sunday July 11 the sun shone through for a brief period at noon and the party made a series of astronomical observations. It was probably at this time that Hime took his photograph of Fort Ellice from the encampment.

The next day the encampment at Fort Ellice was broken up and the expedition proceeded westward at about 5 pm. Heading along the south side of the valley of the Qu'Appelle they travelled steadily along undulating terrain for six days amid continuing inclement weather and troublesome clouds of mosquitoes. Just before sunset on Saturday, July 17 they reached the new Church of England missionary post at the Fishing Lakes and camped on the north side of the Valley. Sunday, the expedition attended Divine Service, rested, and made the usual observations for latitude and variation that evening. The following day the men were back at work 'triangulating to establish the position of prominent points, making a section of valley, levelling the river, taking photographs, and preparing for canoe voyages up and down the Qu'Appelle'.[18]

Hind was most enthusiastic about Hime's photographic work at this point, noting in his report that 'two excellent photographs, taken near the Mission, of the lakes and hills, display the chief characteristics of the valley with the fidelity which can only be attained by that wonderful art'.[19]

As the Qu'Appelle Valley appeared to be a potentially important area it was determined that the expedition 'explore the whole valley from the South Branch of the Saskatchewan to the Assiniboine, and ascertain the relation it bore to these two rivers'.[20] The canoes were put in order and the party and supplies divided for various reconnaissance trips.

Hind and Fleming were to ascend the Qu'Appelle by canoe to its source and follow up the valley of the south branch of the Saskatchewan. Dickinson with the French-Canadian and a Cree half-breed was to descend the Qu'Appelle from the First Fishing Lake to the river's mouth and from there proceed by land to Fort Pelly. Another party with three carts was to proceed along the south side of the Qu'Appelle Valley to meet Hind's canoe division at the Grand Forks of the river. Hime, with four men, carts and Dickinson's supplies was to proceed westerly to Long or Last Mountain Lake and then return in a north-easterly direction to Fort Pelly where he was to meet Dickinson's party. By 3:00 am on the morning of July 20 the parties were underway.

This stage of the exploration provides a closer insight into Hime's personal efforts.

As leader of a survey party he was now obliged to keep a notebook recording progress and observations on each day's trek. Fortunately, this notebook has survived. [21] The notebook reveals many aspects of the journey from Qu'Appelle Mission by way of Long Lake to Fort Pelly. With a neat legible style Hime recorded the fauna, flora and topographical features along the route. He moved his party at a steady pace across a terrain alternating between rolling prairie, marshy lowlands, and gravelly rocky hills during weather that for the most part was inclement and wet.

The first day his party camped at 7:40 pm. The next morning they were on their way at 3:50 am and travelled until 8:30 pm. On July 22 they left at 3:38 am and camped at 7:20 pm. At the end of that day Hime wrote 'Camped. Eat Eaglets for supper as we had nothing else. Musquitos very bad. Thunderstorm.'[22] The following day the party left at 5:20 am. They later met and joined a cart train of HBC men going to Fort Pelly with provisions. On July 24 they left at 5:15 am, stopped for a dinner of skunk and dried meat, and travelled the rest of the day through ponds and stinking pools and swarms of grasshoppers. The next two days they continued their journey through marshy places, by small lakes, and over rolling prairie.

On July 27 the day was to begin badly. Breaking camp at 6:10 am the party first had to cross the White Sand River. Here, the trouble began. Hime recorded the events as follows:

the bank here is steep + high about 50 ft above water – whitish clay wooded with small Pop + Will – on the other side the bank is low wooded with low Will bushes – the river here is rapid running at the rate of about 5 miles per hour + about 11 1/2 ft deep – on account of the unusual deepness of the water had to go about 60 yards higher up river than old crossing where the bank is low similar to opposite side – The course of river is from N to W to S to E – Staged up carts + with another rope before + men on other side to haul proceeded across – the first cart upset in the rapid + I had the satisfaction of seeing my Photographic Apparatus, my gun, my clothes and all my Penates submerged, fortunately they were tied tight and did not get out of the cart – After about 10 minuits struggling the horse was loosed from the cart + swam down the River while the cart was dragged ashore – Got all the other carts across safely before 10 o.c.a.m. – with no accident except one of my men cutting his foot badly on a sharp stone – it was well we were with the Co's men as either party without the other would have found great difficulty in crossing – Stopped to dry the things which although soaked were not much damaged. [23]

Here very graphically are revealed some of the perils of a photographer in the 1850s.

21 Public Archives of Manitoba Collection: Hind, Henry Youle; Assiniboine & Saskatchewan Exploring Expedition. Notebook No 5 kept by H. L. Hime, July 20–27, 1858, and James A. Dickinson, August 27–September 1, 1858. Mission to Fort Pelly and White Mud River Road.
22 *Ibid*, p. x.
23 *Ibid*, pp. xxvi-xxvii.

This unfortunate upset might also explain the very heavy staining and deterioration which appears on the Qu'Appelle Lakes photograph. Quite possibly this negative had been uppermost in the box and thus was watersoaked.

At 1:50 in the afternoon the party was again underway. By 4:25 they crossed the Assiniboine and ten minutes later were at Fort Pelly. Hime's division had completed its survey work in seven days. During this time Hime was probably too preoccupied to have taken any photographs. Certainly the weather had been bad during most of the trip.

At Fort Pelly, Hime and his men had some five days to rest while awaiting the arrival of Dickinson's party. Hime was probably anxious to test his photographic apparatus as soon as possible following its upset on July 27. That all was in good order is evidenced by the two excellent views of the Fort Pelly buildings which he succeeded in taking.

Dickinson joined Hime on August 1. The next day they made the usual observations to determine latitude and magnetic variations. On August 3 they made a short traverse to the Swan River some 9½ miles to the north. A little past noon they set out on horseback with a Mr Macdonald who was in charge at the Fort. They travelled along the valley of the Snake Creek to its confluence with the Swan River. Having ascertained the dimensions of the Swan and its valley they returned to Fort Pelly.

The following morning the party left Fort Pelly heading south-east along the left bank of the Assiniboine with the intention of exploring the country between the river and the Duck and Riding Mountains. The journey was relatively uneventful. The party was preoccupied with taking note of the topography and fording the numerous rivers and creeks. During this journey Dickinson found Hime to be of 'great assistance' in making the survey. On August 7 and 8 a reconnaissance was made up the Shell River. The next day they passed the river trail diverging to Fort Ellice and took the mountain trail along the flanks of the Riding Mountains. At sunset on August 11 the party reached the banks of the Little Saskatchewan or Rapid River and set up camp. The next day the party made the usual observations in the morning, but did little else as the skies grew cloudy and a thunderstorm began.

On August 13, Hime accompanied Dickinson on a horseback reconnoitre some fifteen miles up the Rapid River. As dense woods barred further progress they returned to camp. The next day the party headed south down the Valley of the Rapid. By 3:40 pm on August 15 they had reached the White Mud River trail crossing. Here they stopped to make new axle trees. The following morning Dickinson (and probably Hime) left the men and continued down the valley of the Rapid to its confluence with the Assiniboine. They camped there on the evening of August 17, made a reconnaissance, and began the return journey the next day. At 6:20 pm on August 19 they rejoined their men.

On the morning of August 20 the Dickinson and Hime parties headed west along the White Mud trail towards Fort Ellice. Along the way they surveyed Shoal Lake and the trail, reaching the banks of the Assiniboine near the mouth of Beaver River, a short distance from Fort Ellice about noon on August 23. Here they rejoined Hind's division which had just arrived from Fort à la Corne on the North Saskatchewan. Fleming with his canoe party was not to join them until their return to the Red River Settlements. He was now proceeding by way of the Saskatchewan and Lake Winnipeg.

The reunited divisions struck camp early on the morning of August 24 and commenced eastward along the White Mud trail. They spent the first two days making a section of the Valley in the vicinity of Fort Ellice. By August 27 the expedition was some fifty miles from the fort. When they rose that morning it was noted that there was ice on the water and tents were frozen. It was getting late in the season for men who had been equipped for a summer expedition. The primary objective would now be to get back to the Settlements as soon as possible.

On August 31 they had reached the elbow of the White Mud River where it turned northward to empty into Lake Manitoba. Hind sent Dickinson on a short canoe survey down the River to its mouth. He himself followed later on horseback to bring back the canoe. Meanwhile, Hime took the remaining carts and proceeded some five miles along the trail and then camped to await the return of the others. The next day the party reached Prairie Portage and camped for the night. The following morning they were bound for the Red River Settlements via Lanes's Post and the White Horse Plain trail along the north side of the Assiniboine. On September 4 the expedition reached Fort Garry after an absence of three months.

The main work was now completed. A vast amount of information pertaining to the geology, topography, natural history and meteorology of the Assiniboine and Saskatchewan area had been procured. In all, the expedition had travelled over 2220 miles. Hind and his men must have been satisfied with their efforts. They were fortunate to have suffered no serious calamities and to have completed their exploration in relatively good time with few delays. Perhaps only the bad weather, the grasshoppers and the mosquitoes were to be regretted.

Hime had certainly done his share of the work. He had looked after the train, assisted commendably in the survey work, and had successfully led his own survey party to Long Lake and Fort Pelly. He had travelled some 1170 miles. But in fulfilling his primary role as expedition photographer he had had only limited success. The harshness of the weather had dogged his efforts. Moreover, the rigid timetable of the journey had severely limited his opportunities for photography.

Just how many photographs he did manage to take during those three months is unknown. He had taken at least two hundred glass-plates with him to Red River. However, the fact that only eight photos taken during the June to September journey into the interior have survived suggests that he had used very few. Even these eight were not representative of the work he was capable of producing. They did not compare with the work he had done on the way to Red River during the previous May and June. They lacked clarity, sharpness and good processing. However, the shortcomings of these photographs is to be attributed not to Hime's inability to handle the apparatus, but rather to limitations in the equipment and in the very process of collodion wet-plate photography.

The limitations of the camera lenses were recognized as a drawback on other photographic expeditions of the 1850s. Captain J.H. Simpson, who had conducted an exploration of the Great Basin of Utah for the United States in 1859 noted in his official report that his photographers had had limited success and that he was informed that in several other government expeditions photography had failed. He went on to state that

the cause lies in some degree in the difficulty in the field, at short notice, of having preparations perfect enough to secure good pictures, but chiefly in the fact that the camera is not adapted to distant scenery. For objects very close at hand, which of course, correspondingly contracts the field of vision, and for single portraits of persons and small groups, it does very well, but on exploring expeditions ... the camera has to be correspondingly distant to take in the whole field, and the consequence is a want of sharpness of outline and in many instances, on account of the focal distance not being the same for every object within the field of view, a blurred effect, as well as distortion of parts. [24]

But perhaps the most significant factor was the limitation in the techniques and processes of wet-plate collodion photography. In 1858 these had not yet been so fully developed as to provide maximum results under the conditions met in the Western Interior. Too little was known of exposure times. Hardwich's manual of photography offerred only general guidelines based mainly on experience in Europe and in the tropics. Moreover, the chemistry of wet-plate photography was limited. It worked well under controlled conditions, but was unpredictable and often unstable when variants in environment and chemical composition were introduced.

Hime's expedition photography was often performed under conditions beyond his control. The chemical processing was accomplished in the open, subject to the existing temperature and humidity situations which could hardly be regulated. Moreover, Hime had to rely on local water supplies which often must have been far from ideal for photo-

24 Taft, Robert; *Photography and the American Scene: A Social History, 1839-1889*, (New York, Dover Publications, Inc. 1964) p.267.

graphic purposes. These factors were perhaps the main determinants in the quality of his photographs. The decomposition evident in some of them is probably due in part to impurities in the water and to the fact that temperature conditions were not adequate as much as it was due to poor washing procedures.

In the final analysis Hime was probably disappointed with his photographic work in the field. But now that he was back at Red River he would have an opportunity to prove himself as a master of the camera.

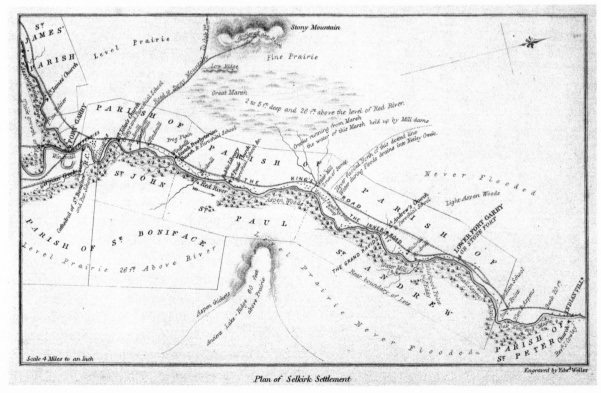

Plan of Selkirk Settlement

CHAPTER VI

Hime and his photography

at Red River:

September 4–November 30

25 Hind, North-West Territory Reports ..., *op. cit.*, p. 15.

26 It is not known if Hime made any prints from the negatives while he was at Red River. He did have a supply of photographic print paper, but this was listed as being packed in a cardboard box and left at Red River with the rest of the photographic apparatus. PAC, RG 5, C 1, Vol. 578, 1858, Red River Exploration No. 1718, Inventory of Property ... *op. cit.*

27 The original portrait submitted with the official series to the Canadian Government in 1859 is captioned 'Jane L'Adamar'. However, the portraits prepared in 1860 for the published portfolio are captioned 'Susan: A Swampy-Cree half-breed'. As the original portrait was made by Hime or his colleague Beere soon after the Expedition, and as there is an entry in the St Andrew's Parish Marriage Register 1860–1883 #315 (Manitoba Archives) listing in 1860 a Jane Ladimar, servant, age 18, it is reasonable to assume that the portrait is that of Jane L'Adamar.

The expedition found plenty to do at Red River that September. Hind spent a fortnight writing reports and making preparations for a canoe voyage through Lake Winnipeg, the Little Saskatchewan River and Lake Manitoba to the Salt Regions on the shores of Lake Winnipegosis. Dickinson prepared for a further exploration of the country between Lake of the Woods and Red River and between the Assiniboine and the 49th parallel. On September 16 Fleming's party returned from Fort à la Corne. Two days later Hind and Fleming set out for Lake Winnipeg and beyond. Dickinson left the same day to explore the country east and west of Red River. He would not return until October 20. Hind and Fleming were gone until the 31st.

During the absence of his colleagues Hime remained at Red River occupying his time, as the official report states, '... in executing a number of photographs of scenes, churches, buildings, Indians, etc, which will form an interesting collection'.[25] He now had the time and freedom of action necessary for good photography. He could wait until the weather was favourable. He could set up his apparatus with care, be meticulous in the preparation of his chemicals, choose his subjects, and take his exposures at his leisure.

Hime took at least three dozen photographs at Red River.[26] Most were taken on clear bright days, probably in September and early October as he wandered between the Lower Fort, the Middle and Upper Settlements, and along the banks of the Red and Assiniboine. Thirty-five of these photographs have survived. They are superb photographs, revealing not only the skill of the photographer in processing, but his mastery of composition and intuitive inventiveness in making use of external settings for portraits.

These Red River photographs, moreover, were exactly what was required for expedition purposes. Six of them exhibit the general character of the river and the level country through which it flows. Another fifteen clearly reveal the architecture of the churches, houses, stores, HBC buildings, and Forts. There are four excellent views of Indian graves and tents and one close-up of a Blackfoot Robe. There are also five portraits of Red River inhabitants – John McKay, Wigwam, Letitia, Jane L'Adamar, and an Ojibway woman with papoose. These are perhaps Hime's best works. The portraits of Wigwam and of the Ojibway woman reveal a mastery of classic studio composition. Those of Jane L'Adamar (whose portrait has often been wrongly captioned as Susan, a Swampy Cree half-breed)[27] and John McKay, on the other hand, show a spontaneous capturing of character and spirit without any posing of the subject. The portrait of Letitia is unique, being neither totally posed nor wholly spontaneous, but a clever natural arrangement of the subject in an external setting. Indeed, Hime's photography at Red River was an unqualified success.

The expeditionary party remained at Red River until the end of November although all exploratory work had been completed in October. During the final weeks the geological

and natural history specimens were probably labelled and packed, the observations tabulated, and preliminary maps compiled. Hind and Dickinson worked on their progress reports. An inventory of the remaining supplies and equipment was drawn up and arrangements made to leave most of the material with two merchants of Red River until it could be shipped out the following spring. This inventory included most of the apparatus with the exception of the negatives taken at Red River. These, Hime was to take with him. He was also instructed to take with him the negatives of the Souris, Assiniboine, and Qu'Appelle. But for some unexplained reason, which Hind later interpreted as being in direct opposition to his expressed wishes, Hime left these particular negatives at Red River and, to Hind's further consternation, was later to forget exactly where he had packed them.

The last week of November final arrangements were made for the winter journey from Red River to St Paul, Minnesota. The parties were to travel by nine dog carioles along the snow trail to Crow-Wing some 400 miles to the south. All was in readiness for an early morning start on Tuesday, November 30. That morning Hime was to take his final photograph at Red River. He set up his camera and took a view of three of the departing carioles. Then, completing his processing, Hime packed away the last of his equipment and sped off to join his colleagues on the trail. On December 13 the expedition reached Crow-Wing, then travelled by stagecoach to La Crosse on the Mississippi and boarded a train for the East. Within a week they were back in Toronto.

Hime probably felt that he had acquitted himself well on the expedition. Unfortunately, his superior officer, Hind, did not share the same view. Initially, in his preliminary reports and letters he had on occasion praised Hime's efforts. But at a later date he was to express strong dissatisfaction with Hime. In the introduction to the official published report Hind lauded the excellent qualities of Dickinson and Fleming and then went on to say

Who can conceive the pain and anxiety which the absence or temporary suppression of these qualities in a companion is capable of inflicting, when circumstances will not permit avoidance or separation...[28]

This condemnation Hind later pointed out was directed towards Hime who Hind considered had 'neglected his duty, and proved a very undesirable companion on an expedition of this kind, retarding its progress and work'.[29] He did not amplify or justify this charge. Perhaps he felt that Hime had spent too much time on photography with too few tangible results and should have been doing more survey work. Or perhaps he felt that Hime had not taken a sufficient number of photographs. Probably Hind never came to appreciate the difficulties of photography, the exactness, the tediousness, the time involved, and the conditions so necessary to achieve good results.

CHAPTER VII

The expedition's official
reports and photographs

28 Hind, North-West Territory Reports ..., *op. cit*
Introduction, p. vi.

29 PAC, RG 5, C I, Vol. 707, 1862, No. 557. H.Y.
Hind to Prov. Secretary, June 20, 1862.

30 PAC, RG 5, C I, Vol. 707, 1862, No. 557. H.Y.
Hind to Prov. Secretary, June 20, 1862.

31 The making of positive proofs and prints in the
1850s could be undertaken in a number of ways,
using a variety of materials and techniques. See
Part III

32 PAC, RG 5, C I, Vol. 578–579, 1858, Red River
Exploration, No. 1718, No. 174. H.Y. Hind to
C. Alleyn, Provincial Secretary, Feb. 2, 1859.

Back in Toronto the members of the expedition immediately began to prepare the final reports, maps and illustrations. That is, all the members with the apparent exception of Hime. According to Hind 'Mr. Hime absented himself without leave for ten days after our arrival and at subsequent periods, until the close of his connection with the expedition, occasionally for a day or two.'[30] As far as Hind was concerned Hime had 'neglected his duty and amused himself in the country' while the others were hard at work all the time. However, Hind's opinion of Hime's behaviour is open to question as it was given some two years later, on June 20, 1862 after Hind had had some rather bitter dealings with Hime and his associates Armstrong and Beere. Whatever the true situation, Hime did continue to complete his photographic work for the expedition. By February 2, 1859 he had prepared trial proofs of his photographs and was working on a set of prints by the time the trial proofs were submitted to the Governor General in Council on February 4.[31]

When Hind submitted Hime's trial proofs on February 2, he made the rather incongruous statement that the photographs 'do not represent Mr Hime's duties in connection with the expedition' and that 'being by profession a surveyor he gave material assistance to Mr Dickinson in the Survey of the Flanks of the Riding Mountains and elsewhere'.[32] It is not known why Hind should make such a statement when in all previous correspondence he had stated that Hime was a photographer, and Hime's official acceptance of the position clearly indicated that his primary duties were to be those of photographer. Perhaps this refusal to recognize Hime as a Photographer was an expression of Hind's displeasure with the man and his disappointment in Hime's photographic efforts.

Whatever the case, some time in early March Hind requested that Hime have the set of final prints prepared sooner than was first intended. Hime agreed to get the job done and apparently had the prints completed on the specified date. However, to meet the new deadline Hime employed his associate, Mr Beere, to assist him in the work.

This hiring of Beere proved to be a bone of contention between Hime and Hind. It led to bitterness and a disagreement which unfortunately was to last for several years. Hime believed that Hind had agreed to the employment of Beere at the same rate of pay as himself. Hind, on the other hand, contended that Hime had hired Beere on his own authority which he had no right to do. He apparently was willing to accept Hime's action, but changed his mind when the firm of Armstrong, Beere and Hime submitted their bill on May 4 for the sum of $80.00 as a charge for Beere's services which they stated had been for one month. Hind refused to recognize the charge, particularly since he claimed that Hime had informed him on May 6 that Beere had worked only a fortnight. Moreover, Hind later asserted that he was none too sympathetic towards the claim because he felt that Hime had neglected his duty on the expedition. As a result, at some later date that year he submitted a modified claim to the Provincial Secretary for payment of $40.00 to cover Beere's service.

By October 14 Armstrong, Beere and Hime had not yet been reimbursed and Hime wrote a letter to Hind enquiring when the bill was to be paid and pointing out that he had paid cash for all the photographic materials. The firm received no satisfaction. On November 12 Armstrong, on behalf of the firm, wrote to the Assistant Secretary for an answer. There was still no satisfaction. Finally, on April 2, 1860, Hind paid the firm $40.00 to cover the charges. The firm was displeased and wrote Hind for an explanation. Receiving no answer they then directed another enquiry to the Assistant Secretary on April 11. On April 21 Hind wrote to Hime and disclaimed any knowledge of Beere's claim for the additional fortnight, but indicated a willingness to listen to the case. Hime was persistent and Hind wrote again on April 30 stating that if Hime persisted he would forward the claim to the Provincial Secretary, but warned that little good would come of it. In reply Hime wrote that it was a matter of indifference to him if Hind submitted the claim to the Provincial Secretary for he looked to Hind alone for payment.

Eventually the firm took legal action and sued Hind. The Division Court, according to Hind, dismissed the case. According to the firm, the Court had decided that they 'must look to the Government for payment'. [33] As a final effort the firm then applied on April 22, 1862 to the Provincial Secretary. Hind was once again asked to state his views to the Provincial Secretary and he did so in bitter language on June 20, 1862. On July 7 the Governor-General in Council rejected the firm's claim. There is no evidence that the firm pursued the matter any further. By this time Hime had left the firm and it was probably decided that any further action was hopeless.

Returning to the activities of the expedition in 1859, we see that by March 28 the preliminary Report was ready and progress was being made on the remaining reports, the maps and illustrations. Every effort was being made to complete the work of the expedition. On April 16 Hind requested permission to write to McDermot at Red River informing him to send by cart to St Paul and hence to Toronto by express 'the geological specimens, the Photographic Negatives left behind and apparatus, with the more valuable instruments'. Hind indicated that he required the geological specimens to enable him to continue his report and that he was concerned that the photographic apparatus and negatives would be spoiled if left much longer where they were at Red River. [34] The negatives to which Hind referred were those taken on the Souris, the Assiniboine and Qu'Appelle which Hime had left behind at the Settlements. They apparently never did arrive in Toronto that year for by August 17 Hind had received the geological specimens and survey instruments, but not the negatives. The box in which they were stated to have been placed arrived, but without containing them.

33 PAC, RG 5, C I, Vol. 707, 1862, No. 557. Armstrong and Beere late Armstrong, Beere, & Hime to the Offiice of the Provincial Secretary, April 22, 1862.

34 PAC, RG 5 C I, Vol. 578–579, 1858 Red River Exploration, No. 1718, No. 721. H.Y. Hind to C. Alleyn, April 16, 1859.

By April 20, copies of all the reports were ready and submitted to the Legislative Assembly for its consideration. Arrangements were then made to have the reports printed. On August 17, Hind reported that the maps were nearly all lithographed, the preliminary reports were printed, and the General Report partly printed. Twenty watercolours had also been completed and copies of the photographs were ready for the Provincial Exhibition.

The photographs were put on display in the Fine Arts Section of the Provincial Exhibition when it was held in Kingston between September 27–30. They were duly noted in the press, but there was no mention of them in the prize lists.

Other copies of the photographs were also prepared about this time and forwarded to the Colonial Secretary, the Duke of Newcastle, later in the fall.

By the end of September the work of the Assiniboine and Saskatchewan Exploring Expedition was brought to a close. The final accounts had been submitted and the staff discharged. All the reports, tables, lithographs, maps, and a list of photographs were then officially published as a Government Blue Book.

The Blue Book and the results of the expedition attracted some attention. The Canadian press generally published notices and extracts from the reports. Some Canadian journals criticized the expedition for giving little positive information although $50,000 to $60,000 had been expended for the purpose. It was claimed that the country had been better explored previously by the astronomer Thompson. However, Dr Petermann, an American and 'well known authority amongst geographers' published a defence of the expedition. He asserted that the expedition 'excited the curiosity of the people more than that of Capt. Palliser', that a society had been formed at St Paul with the objective of exploring the valleys and sources of the Saskatchewan and Columbia Rivers, that the St Paul Board of Trade was offering a $1,000 reward for the first steamer to ply the Red River on or before the first of June, and that another company in Canada intended to put four steamers on Rainy Lake, Red River and Lake Winnipeg. [35] The *Canadian Journal of Science, Literature and History*, the official publication of the Canadian Institute, also favourably reviewed the reports. The British Government was sufficiently interested in the reports of the expedition to have them reissued in London in August of 1860. But as the *Canadian Journal* was later to point out

Parliament can print blue books, but it is beyond its power to make people read them; and we doubt if the 'Red River' (Official Report on the 1857 Expedition) and 'Assiniboine' Blue Books furnished any very notable exception to this dictum. Extracts and digests in the periodical press sufficed to gratify popular enquiry; a few copies were bound and placed on the shelves of both public and private libraries, both here and at home, and the remainder, it is to be feared, experienced the usual fate of Blue Books, however valuable. [36]

35 *Canadian Journal of Science, Literature & History*, Series 2, Vol. v, 1860, p.550.
36 *Canadian Journal of Science, Literature & History*, Series 2, Vol. vi, 1861, p.175.

CHAPTER VIII

The Hind volumes and the
photograph portfolio of 1860

37 Hind, *Narrative of the Canadian Red River Exploring Expedition ... op. cit.* Vol. 2. Appendix XIV, pp.434–436. The portfolio was entitled *Photographs Taken at Lord Selkirk's Settlement on the Red River of the North to Illustrate a Narrative of the Canadian Exploring Expeditions in Rupert's Land.* London, J. Hogarth, 1860.

38 PAC, MG 24, E 17.2, Sir Ed. Watkin Papers. A printed pamphlet, *Narrative ..., op. cit.* p.2.

39 PAC, MG 24, E 17.2, Sir Ed. Watkin Papers. A printed pamphlet, *Narrative ..., op. cit.* p.5

40 *Ibid*, p.7.

41 *Ibid*, p.9.

Professor Hind was convinced that the subjects of the Expeditions of 1857 and 1858 merited a wider and more enduring interest. Therefore, he set out to write for publication a further account of these two expeditions. This account was published by the end of 1860 in two handsome volumes by the London firm of Longman, Green, Longman and Roberts under the title *Narrative of the Canadian Red River Exploring Expedition of 1857 and of the Assiniboine and Saskatchewan Exploring Expedition of 1858*. The volumes contained 996 pages and sold for two Guineas in Britain and $12.00 in Canada. The text was almost entirely a verbatim copy of all the official reports that Hind had submitted to the Canadian Government. However, the text was accompanied by approximately one hundred illustrations. These illustrations were acknowledged to be from sketches by John Fleming and from photographs taken by Humphrey Lloyd Hime.

Whatever Hind thought about the efforts of his photographer on that expedition of 1858 he was well aware of the quality and value of the photographs. Not only were seven of the full page chromoxylygraphs, including the frontispiece of volume II and seven of the woodcuts copied from Hime's views, but a separate portfolio of Hime photographs was published by J. Hogarth, 5 Haymarket, London to supplement the two volumes. [37]

This portfolio consisted of a selection of thirty 6 x 8 prints of the photographs taken at Red River. They were finely mounted, captioned and sold for two Guineas for the series. The prints themselves were probably made from the original negatives.

It is unlikely that the portfolio prints were made by Hime. Probably the negatives had been sent to Great Britain with the approval of the Canadian Government to be printed by a British photographic firm. If this was the case it might explain the fact that no original Hime negatives have been found in Canada.

Although no contemporary comments on the portfolio have been located there is a wealth of evidence that the two Hind volumes were well received by the British press. The *Morning Post*, January 7, 1861, declared

To the general reader, it will prove attractive for its varied and pleasing descriptions of places and scenes in the far-distant West ... To the emigrant, proposing to seek his fortune in the backwoods of the West, it is invaluable for its clear elucidation of the resources of those interminable tracts ... But it is to the Government, both Canadian and British, that the information contained in these volumes is most valuable. It points out the means how ... a vast tract of land ... may be made a chain of communication from one side of the continent to the other. [38]

The publication *John Bull*, January 19, 1861, stated 'that the reader has before him one of the most important contributions that have been made for many years to our commercial

and political knowledge'.[39] The *Oriental Budget*, January 1860, remarked that Hind 'did his duty discreetly and earnestly. He has now afforded the world an opportunity of obtaining in London, what they might have difficulty in procuring from the archives of Toronto'.[40] And *The Atheneum*, December 22, 1860, offered the praise that the volumes were 'creditable to Mr Hind and his brother explorers'.[41]

But as these accolades rolled from the press Hind and 'his brother explorers' had moved on to other tasks and pursuits.

CHAPTER IX

The subsequent career of Humphrey Lloyd Hime

Hime rejoined his partners Armstrong and Beere immediately after the expedition work was completed. He was to stay with them for several years, although by 1861 he had also begun a career in finance. On October 25 of that year he attended one of the first meetings of the Toronto Stock Exchange; it is recorded in the minutes that he was one of the brokers instrumental in drawing up a series of rules and regulations. By 1864 he had discontinued his connection with Armstrong and Beere and become a broker and commission agent with an office in the Masonic Hall. He served as treasurer of the Royal Canadian Yacht Club from 1864 to 1868. In 1865 he became vice-president of the Toronto Stock Exchange. He took an active interest in mining on the north shore of Lake Superior in 1867. In the next two years he served as president of the Stock Exchange and extended his personal business into real estate and insurance.

Hime married prior to 1861. He and his wife Christina were to have eight children. [42] The family lived for many years on Robert Street and later moved to Wellington Place. The Himes belonged to the Church of England and were active members of St Stephen-in-the-Fields on Bellevue Avenue. In 1872 Hime served as a lay member of Synod for Toronto-St Stephen's.

In 1873 Hime entered municipal politics, running as aldermanic representative for St Patrick's ward. The *Globe* stated that his election would be highly advantageous to Council as he was a man of education who had large interests in the ward. The voters heeded the advice. At the inaugural meeting of City Council Hime was named a member of the Finance and Assessment Standing Committee, the Board of Health Committee, and the Jail Committee. His appointment to the Finance Committee was challenged, but he was ably defended on the grounds that his business and financial ability eminently fitted him to be a member of that committee. Hime served on City Council for one year and then retired from municipal politics. In 1874 he was appointed Justice of the Peace. In subsequent years City Council occasionally called upon him for financial advice and assistance in real estate matters.

In 1891 Hime was a fairly prominent citizen in Toronto. He had served again as president of the Stock Exchange in 1888-89. He was also president of the Copeland Brewing Company, a director of the Toronto Belt Line Railway and Belt Land Corporation, and a director of the Northland Railway Company. Although he had formerly been connected with the Reform Association, he now took no active part in politics. He was also head of the firm of Messrs H.L. Hime and Company, stock brokers, real estate and insurance agents. His real estate holdings included substantial property in Toronto, Sault Ste Marie, Orillia, Thunder Bay, and in the Muskoka, Simcoe and Algoma regions.

On Saturday, October 31, 1903 Hime died. He was survived by his wife and seven of

42 Frederick Clifford (born Sept. 10, 1861), Ethel Mary (born Sept. 25, 1863), Arthur Gilmor (born July 18, 1865), Maud Emily (born Oct. 4, 1867), Francis Charles (born June 1, 1870), Walter Lloyd (born May 5, 1873), Maurice William (born Oct. 17, 1875), Marion Christine (born April 13, 1879).

43 By 1903 Frederick had died. Walter and Maurice had taken over some of their father's business. Arthur, Francis, and Ethel were living in the Hawaiian Islands. Maud had married and was living in Toronto while Marion was still at home with her mother.

44 *The Globe*, Toronto, Monday, November 2, 1903, p. 10.

45 For an inventory of known Hime photographs see appendix II.

his children. [43] He was given a private funeral and was eulogized by his contemporaries as 'one of the best known and most highly esteemed agents in Toronto'. [44]

There is no record of Hime practicing photography during his last thirty years. Probably he abandoned it when he left the firm of Armstrong and Beere and turned to finance. But it is not for his financial successes that history remembers Hime. It is for his pioneer work as a photographer in the Western Interior. The photographs he took in 1858 have been his enduring monument. [45]

Appendix 1

Inventory of property, belonging to the 'Assiniboine and Saskatchewan Exploring Expedition' left at Selkirk Settlement, Red River, in charge of Andrew McDermot, Nov. 1858.

Photographic Apparatus   –   in Box marked   D

1 Camera complete, with 2 inch portrait & landscape lenses & field f x 7¹/₄ –
2 Porcelain Dishes
1 Wooden   D° glass Bottom
2 Tandishes – 1 glass & 1 gutta percha
2 Glass measures – 12 oz & 1 minim
1 Box of scales and weights
1 Pint bottle of Iodized Collodion
1 Pint of Collodion in 2 pint Bots.
2 4 oz glass stoppered bottles – empty
1 4 oz Bottle glacial acetic acid
1 oz Anthony's Diamond varnish
4 oz whiting
1 Pint Bot. glass stop. – empty
2 oz Bot. Carb. soda
4 8 gr Bots. chloride gold
2 oz gallic acid
1 4 oz Bot. Copal varnish
1 4 oz Bot. glass stop. – empty
1 Pint   D°   D°
1 Card Box with 100 sqrs Photoᶜ. Paper
5 Linen Rubbers
2 Silk D°
1 Bottle 4 oz Cleaning liquid
1 Bradall

Contents of Box Marked E

2 Pints Ether
1 D°   Alcohol
2 D°   Nitrate Silv. Bath

Carried over

Photograph   Apparatus –   in Box   E

1 Pint Bt. – Empty
1 4 oz Bot. Cyenide of Potassium – $1/2$ full
1 D°   D°   acetic acid
1 D°   D°   Iodide Potassium – $1/2$ full
1 D°   D°   Pyrogallic acid   nearly full
1 Tin Canister containing about 3 oz gun cotton
About $1/2$ lb Nitrate Silver
1 4 oz Bot. Empty
1 spare Dark Slide for Camera
1 Gutta Percha Bath – horizontal
1 Patent filter
2 oz white glue
Hardwick's *Manual of Phot^c. Chemistry*

Contents of Box marked   F

About 220 sheets of glass for Camera
   " $1/2$ lb Hyposulphite soda in pt. bot.
1–6 oz Bot. Nit. Silv. sensit.   . S 1.
1 Pint Bot. glass stop. – empty
1 D°   D°
2 Files
4 Box hooks
6 eyes
1 small brass *hinge* for Camera

Sundries

1 Dark tent and poles
1 linen rybber – inside tent
12 Clothes pins   – " –
1 Pewter tap, 1 sqr Ind. rub. 1.2 gal. keg
1 sugar keg –

Total   250.00

31

Appendix II

An Inventory of Known

Hime Photographs

The photographs reproduced and listed in Part One are all the images known to have been taken by Humphrey Lloyd Hime at the time of the Assiniboine and Saskatchewan Exploring Expedition of 1858 and that now exist as original prints or as contemporary artistic reproductions in the *Illustrated London News* and in H.Y. Hind's, *Narrative of the Canadian Red River Exploring Expedition of 1857 and of the Assinboine and Saskatchewan Exploring Expedition of 1858* (London, 1860). There is no evidence that the original glass plate negatives have survived and no further contemporary reproductions can be attributed to Hime's photographic images.

The Public Archives of Canada possesses original photographic prints of numbers 13 to 25, 27 to 40, 43 to 48, which were prepared by H.L. Hime and D. Beere in February–March, 1859. These prints formed part of the official report submitted to the Canadian Government in 1859 by the Assiniboine and Saskatchewan Exploring Expedition. The prints are mounted and captioned. On some of the prints H.L. Hime's signature appears at the bottom. The mounts are embossed in the lower left corner with the stamp of the firm of Armstrong, Beere and Hime. Bound with this series are original photographic prints of numbers 3, 4, 5 to 12, and 41 which are also mounted and captioned but bear no embossed stamp of the firm nor any signature. These latter prints were probably prepared at a later date for the Government but not necessarily by H.L. Hime. In this series is also a mounted print of number 49 which is signed by H.L. Hime but the mount is not embossed with the name of the firm. (Public Archives of Canada Historical Photographs Collection Accession No 1970–88).

The Public Archives of Canada also possesses one complete series of the original photographic prints (numbers 13 to 45, 48) prepared in 1860 and published by J. Hogarth, 5 Haymarket, London as a portfolio entitled *Photographs Taken at Lord Selkirk's Settlement on the Red River of the North to Illustrate a Narrative of the Canadian Exploring Expeditions in Rupert's Land*. The Public Archives of Canada also has a second incomplete series of this portfolio (numbers 14 to 25, 27, 29, 30, 31, 34, 35, 37, 42, 44, 48). The prints for the portfolio are mounted and captioned but unsigned. (Public Archives of Canada Historical Photographs Collection Accession No 1936–273).

The Toronto Public Library, Canadian History and Manuscript Section possesses the only known original photographic print of H.L. Hime's 'Ojibways at Fort Frances' (No 1). This print is included in a series of original signed photographic prints of Hime's photographs (numbers 1, 6, 13 to 40, 42 to 48) mounted and bound in a scrapbook album. The prints are attributed incorrectly as being made by Prof H.Y. Hind. It is more likely that the prints were made and bound for H.Y. Hind as his personal album.

The Provincial Archives of Manitoba has twenty-nine original prints signed by Hime (numbers 3 to 8, 20 to 26, 30 to 32, 34 to 40, 42, 43, 45 to 48) and two unsigned prints (numbers 20 and 29). The Notman Photographic Archives of McCord Museum, Montreal, also has thirty original signed Hime photographs (numbers 13 to 16, 18 to 25, 27 to 30, 32, 34 to 40, 42 to 46, and 48) as well as an unsigned print of number 41. The National Library of Canada possesses volume xxxiii of the *Illustrated London News* which contains the October 16, 1858 issue with two engravings of H.L. Hime's photographs taken on May 24 and June 2, 1858 (numbers 2 and 4). Both the Public Archives of Canada and the National Library of Canada possess several sets of the two volumes of H.Y. Hind's *Narrative of the Canadian Red River Exploring Expedition of 1858 and of the Assiniboine and Saskatchewan Exploring Expedition of 1858*, (London, Longman, Green, Longman and Roberts, 1860). These volumes contain fourteen illustrations copied from H.L. Hime's photographs.

Other Canadian repositories possess original photographic prints of the 1860 portfolio of Hime photographs or reproductions made from the originals. Undoubtedly, a number of Canadian libraries hold issues of the *Illustrated London News* or sets of the 1860 H.Y. Hind volumes which contain reproductions of Hime photographs.

Part III
Landscape Photography in the 1850s

CHAPTER 1

The wet-plate

photographer in the field

In 1851 Frederick Scott Archer, a British sculptor and photographer, introduced a photographic system which was to replace the then popular processes initiated by Daguerre and Fox-Talbot and the more recently invented albumen-on-glass process of Niepce de St. Victor. Although the daguerreotype process produced images of the finest quality and detail, it was limited by the fact that its image was unique and could not be reproduced. Fox-Talbot's Talbotype or Calotype process did produce a negative image from which any number of reproductions could be made, but it suffered from the fact that the negative base was paper and the grain and imperfections of the paper placed limitations on the quality of the final images. Niepce de St. Victor's albumen-on-glass process invented in 1848, also a negative process eliminated through its glass base the imperfections and limitations of the paper base; however, sensitized albumen was slow and required extremely long exposures.

Scott Archer's photographic system, announced in London and published in *The Chemist* in March, 1851, substituted iodized collodion for albumen. Because the process required that the exposure and development be done while the collodion was wet the process became known as the collodion wet-plate process. It had numerous advantages. It was faster than any other then known photographic process and had excellent tonal quality and detail. Moreover, it was an invention freed from commercial restrictions and copyright. Thus, its popularity was almost instantaneous and was not to be superceded for more than thirty years. It was the photographic process of both the portrait and the landscape photographer of the 1850s. [1]

For landscape photography the collodion wet-plate process could produce some spectacular results. But there were some very definite disadvantages. The process necessitated the transporting of a lot of cumbersome equipment and supplies, including not only the camera, lens and plates, but a panoply of chemicals, trays, bottles, and a portable darkroom. Moreover, the processing time in the field was extremely long. Finally, the process was almost totally dependent upon the vagaries of the field environment. But the landscape photographer of the 1850s learned to cope with these drawbacks and limitations until better systems were available to him.

Leaving the comfort of his home the landscape photographer of the 1850s set off with all that was required until he found a promising subject for his camera. Then he began to unpack. There was always some haste, brought about in part by the awareness that at any moment the weather might change. He also unpacked with some trepidation, wondering whether the equipment and supplies had survived the journey. So it was with care and anxiety that everything was unloaded from wagon, boat, back, or whatever means of conveyance had been employed for the occasion.

Once the gear was unloaded the portable darkroom was set up in some cool, shady and

convenient place. Portable darkrooms took on a variety of shapes and composition. They could be as elaborate as converted railway cars or specially designed carriages and carts to be pulled by beast or man. More common was some sort of collapsible tent and pole structure that could be assembled or dismantled in a few moments and carried on a man's back with little inconvenience.

One such tent system, probably typical of portable darkrooms of the 1850s, is described in Hardwich's manual.[2] It consisted of four poles 5/16″ in diameter, each in two parts, fitted together with a friction brass tube. The bottom parts were 41″ in length with iron points to stick in the ground. The top parts were 35″ long and also had an iron point. There was also a shelf consisting of two boards each 30″ x 15″ x 5/16″ hinged together and with holes in the corners to take the four poles. The tent covering usually consisted of two thicknesses of ordinary calico, dyed yellow and formed in the shape of a cube open on one side. That side continued in the shape of a sack, with a cord passing around the opening so as to be able to tighten it around the waist of the operator. The tent could also be lined with an additional thickness of black calico with a square foot aperture cut for a window. In the bottom of the tent were four holes for the poles and another four holes at the top to fit exactly on the pins on the top of the poles. The poles, the shelf, and the covering weighed thirteen pounds and cost 24s 6d to have made in 1857 – 18s for purchase of calico, dying and making up the covers, 3s for carpenter's work, and 3s 6d for other work.

It took three minutes to assemble this portable darkroom tent of Hardwich's. Two people were needed to set it up and adjust the poles. A check was made to see that the tent let in no light and that it was secured. To use the darkroom the photographer put the top part of his body through the opening and had the cord tied tightly around his waist while his arms and upper part of his body remained free to move about within the tent.

The next task was to unpack and inspect the chemicals and apparatus. These items were usually packed in fitted leather or wooden cases lined with green beige. The trough for the Nitrate Bath was in one of these cases. This trough was made either of Gutta Percha, porcelain, or glass with a tight top of caoutchouc.

There was also an assortment of bottles, glasses and implements housing a veritable apothecary's shop of chemicals and supplies. According to Hardwich[3], a photographer going out on a few days trip would need at least the following essentials:

1 full trough of Nitrate Bath	2–3 spare various size stopper bottles
1/2 pint bottle of additional Nitrate Bath	2–3 developing glasses each holding 12 drachms
15 oz of Plain Collodion	a minum measure
5 oz of iodizing solution	Scales and weights

1 Unless otherwise indicated all facts which follow in this chapter are taken from various sections of T.F. Hardwich's *A Manual of Photographic Chemistry Including the Practice of the Collodion Process* (London: John Churchill, 1859) Fifth Edition.
2 Hardwich, *op. cit.*, pp.261–263.
3 Hardwich, *op. cit.*, pp.263–264.

5 oz of Cadium Collodion

1 oz iodizer with Bromide

2 oz of mixed Ether and Alcohol

3 oz of absolute Alcohol

3 oz of Spirits of Wine

$^1/_2$ oz of Pyrogallic Acid

4 oz Glacial Acetic Acid

$^1/_2$ oz Citric Acid

1 oz Sulphite of Iron

8 oz Hyposulphite of Soda

6 oz bottle of saturated Hyposulphite of Soda

a bottle of Varnish

1 drachm carbonate of soda

a 12 oz bottle for Pyrogallic

1 dropping bottle filled with Nitrate Bath solution

2 4 oz stopper bottles

Gutta Percha funnel

12" x 10" Gutta Percha tray

Spare dipper for Nitrate Bath

Broad camel's hair brush

Pneumatic plate holder

$^1/_2$ Quire blotting paper

Linen cloth and leather for polishing

2 hand cloths

1 yd of yellow tammy or calico

1 yd of black calico

1 sponge

Piece of marine glue

Ball of string

and a paper of pins

Each of these items was handled with caution and care. Some were placed on the shelf in the darkroom tent alongside the Nitrate Bath. The rest were left close at hand outside the tent.

Water needed in the darkroom was carried in a gutta-percha bottle or in a tubular vessel having a flexible top made of MacIntosh cloth which was suspended by a ring to the interior of the tent. On longer photographic journeys when the availibility of proper water supplies was uncertain an additional water keg or two would be included as part of the photographer's baggage.

There was of course the all important supply of glass plates. Glass plates were available and used in a variety of sizes depending upon the specifications of the camera and the lens systems employed. The most common were those cut to the more or less standard plate sizes adopted by the daguerreotype artists: whole plate 6$^1/_2$" x 8$^1/_2$", half plate 4$^1/_2$" x 5$^1/_2$"; quarter plate 3$^1/_4$" x 4$^1/_4$", sixth plate 2$^3/_4$" x 3$^1/_4$", ninth plate 2" x 2$^1/_2$". Stereo plates were available in 6$^3/_4$" x 3$^1/_4$" size.[4] Plates exceeding 6$^1/_2$" x 8$^1/_2$" were referred to as Imperial plates and the most common of these were the 10" x 8" and the 12" x 10" but plates of any intermediate size or as large as 36" x 24" also were available commercially.[5] Ordinary window glass was considered inferior as photographic glass since it was likely to contain scratches and irregularities. Photographers preferred to use patent glass or flatted crown glass free from irregularities and roughed at the edges and corners to prevent the emulsion from drawing away from the glass. For field work the supply of glass plates was normally

4 Rudisill, R., *Mirror Image*, (Albuquerque, University of New Mexico Press, 1971), p.278.

5 *Photographic Notes*, Thomas Sutton Editor, (Simpson Low, Son & Co., London) Vol. 6, No. 114, January 1, 1861.

carried in a grooved wooden box with brass handles. This box would be placed near the darkroom tent.

Finally the photographer turned to the most important of his equipment – his camera and its lenses – which were usually carried in two separate leather cases. The most common cameras for landscape purposes in the 1850s were those like the Ottewill Sliding-Box Folding Camera of 1853. It was designed as a convenient portable camera for 8″ x 10″ wet-plates and consisted of two wooden folding compartments, one sliding within the other for focusing. The outer compartment was fixed to the bottom board and had sides which folded inwards and were held rigid by the lens board. The inner compartment also folded inwards and was held right by a light frame at the front and the ground-glass focusing glass at the rear. The front lens panel was provided with vertical and horizontal movements for sky and foreground adjustments to eliminate distortion and the convergence of vertical lines. The Ottewill when folded formed a package 21″ x 13″ x 3″ which was a fairly practical piece of equipment to be carried in a leather case. [6]

Although typical, the Ottewill was but one of a variety of cameras which were basically custom-designed to suit the inventiveness of photographers who were constantly seeking improvements in their equipment. By the late 1850s some cameras were incorporating a bellows system of cloth or leather rather than the sliding-box principle. However, the cameras of this era remained relatively simple instruments. There was no need for shutters. Because of the long exposure necessary the removal and replacement of the lens cover was sufficient. There were no separate view finders or rangefinders as all focusing was done with the ground glass at the back of the camera. Aperture openings were at first controlled by unscrewing the lens and inserting stops of the appropriate size between the lens components though after 1858 photographers used the more convenient Waterhouse stops which eliminated unscrewing the components.

Most cameras were designed to take a single exposure but there were some stereo systems available. These stereo cameras varied in their construction and operation. Some utilized a two lens system exposing two images on one plate. Others used a single lens system that required either moving the lens board or the whole camera for each of the two exposures and utilized either one or two plates. Included with the camera would be a number of accessories – one or more dark slides for holding the glass plate negatives, a focusing screen and focusing glass, a large focusing cloth with string to throw over the camera and operator to cut out excess light when focusing, and perhaps a view meter.

As with cameras, there were variations and improvements in the lens systems adopted by the photographers of the wet-plate period. The achromatised Wollaston meniscus system had proven most successful and suitable during the early years of photography. It

6 Thomas, D.B., *Science Museum Photography Collection*, (London, His Majesty's Stationary Office, 1969) p.9.

consisted of a positive (biconvex) lens of crown glass cemented to a negative (biconcave) lens of flint glass. This combination of lens cancelled chromatic aberrations. The convex crown glass surface was generally placed facing the sensitized plate, although on many of the lenses it was possible to reverse the lens in its mount so that light passed through it in the opposite direction. Stops were usually placed in front of the lens. This system became known as the single landscape and could be used at apertures up to about F/15. and covered a field of about 50°. The position of the stop in relation to the lens allowed for coma correction, but astigmatism was not eliminated until 1888-1892 when glasses of high refractive index with low dispersion became available. The great disadvantage of the single landscape lens was its small aperture requiring long exposures. [7]

For portrait work Joseph Petzval in 1841 had produced a most successful doublet lens system which could be used at apertures as large as F/3.5. This was about twenty times as fast as the single landscape lens. The Petzval system was well corrected for chromatic and spherical aberrations and for coma. However, it suffered from astigmatism and field curvature and was of little value as a landscape lens since it gave good definition only over a small field. [8]

There was a constant search for a lens system of greater versatility. Gradually there evolved the Universal lenses or 'convertible lens systems' consisting of sets of lenses which, by means of interchangeable elements, could provide systems of a variety of focal lengths. Such systems were the 'Photographie à Verres Combinés' made from about 1841 to 1859 and the Derogy Combination Lens. This latter system was introduced in 1858 by E. Derogy of Paris.

It consists of a large portrait lens of the Petzval type, the front component of which can be used alone as a long-focus landscape lens. Two additional thin doublet lenses are supplied in the case, either of which may be inserted inside the main tube for the purpose of slightly increasing or decreasing the focal length. This makes in all six possible arrangements, equivalent to six separate lenses.

The focal length of the whole system is about 17″ with an aperture of F/7. The focal length of the front component alone is 28″. The additional lenses increase or decrease these focal lengths by about 3″ giving the following possible lenses: for portraits, lenses of focal length 14¹/₂″, 17″ or 20″; for landscapes, lenses of focal length 25″, 28″ or 32″. [9]

Universal lens systems like the Derogy systems became quite popular, giving the wet-plate photographer both portrait and landscape versatility in one lens system. This was economical but the troublesome unscrewing and refitting of the glasses often proved inconvenient and the results were not always perfect.

7 Thomas, D.B., *Science Museum Photography Collection*, (London, His Majesty's Stationary Office, 1969) p.27.
8 *Loc. cit.*
9 *Ibid*, p.32.

The chosen lens system was screwed into the camera. The complete apparatus was then set up on a sturdy wooden tripod in the chosen location for the exposure. The photographer made a final check to see that all was in readiness. If so, he began the various manipulations that would hopefully lead to the successful capturing of the elusive image – the freezing of a moment in time.

First the glass plate had to be cleaned. According to Hardwich this was best done by rubbing the plate for a few moments with a tuft of cotton cloth dipped in a solution of Cream of Tripoli powder, spirits of wine and a little ammonia. The plate was then rinsed in plain water, wiped with a dry cloth, and polished with an old silk handkerchief or a piece of well beaten leather. An alternative method was to add 30-40 drops of water to an ounce of collodion, pour a little of this on the glass and rub and clean off with a tuft of wool. In this case no water was necessary. Whatever method was employed it was to be done quickly. Breathing on the polished plate served as a reliable check for cleanliness.

With the plate well cleaned and polished the next task was to coat it with the photographic collodion emulsion which was the vehicle for retaining the sensitive silver salts. Photographic Collodion was a combination of Plain Collodion (Pyroxyline – i.e. cotton and nitrate, sulphuric acid and nitrogen peroxide – in a solution of Alcohol and Ether which on evaporation leaves a transparent layer which adheres to the glass) and an iodide (potassium iodide being best for landscape work, iodide of Cadium best for dull light or interior; iodides of sodium or ammonium sometimes used). Hardwich recommended an iodizer solution of 160 grains of potassium iodide and 10 oz of alcohol of .816. This was combined with the Plain Collodion in the proportions of one part iodizer to three parts Plain Collodion. The best photographic collodion was that of a transparent lemon-yellow or golden-yellow colour with all particles settled on the bottom. If not of these colours there were likely to be imperfect shadows or grey metallic negatives with no depth. Photographic Collodion could be prepared in advance and carried in bottles; but the coating had to be done in the field as the collodion process required a wet-plate.

Coating the plate had to be done slowly. It could be done in white light. Grasping the plate by the corners in a horizontal position, the photographer poured the prepared Photographic Collodion steadily until a circular pool was formed extending nearly to the edges of the plate. He then made the collodion flow to the corners – bottom left, top left, top right – and poured the excess back into the bottle from the bottom right corner. The plate was rocked to make the diagonal flow lines coalesce. The coated plate was then set aside until slightly sticky (neither too moist nor too dry) normally for twenty seconds or ten seconds in hot weather.

The coated plate was now ready for sensitizing in the Nitrate Bath.[10] The Nitrate Bath

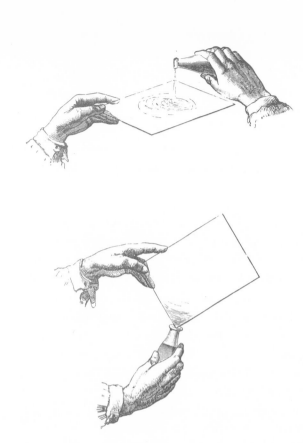

10 Nitrate Baths were the most common although silver iodides, chlorides, or bromides were sometimes used.

41

was usually a combination of silver nitrate (i.e. dissolved metallic silver in nitric acid, which is crystallized by boiling and evaporation) and an equal weight of cold water. Acetic acid or nitric acid or silver acetate were sometimes added. Hardwich recommended a Nitrate Bath composed of 30 grains of recrystallized silver nitrate, $^1/_5$ minn. glacial acetic acid, 15 minn. alcohol, 1 fld oz of distilled water and $^1/_4$ grain of potassium iodide for every 100 grains of silver nitrate. The Nitrate Bath could also be prepared in advance and stored in a bottle. However, the Bath was sometimes a problem for the landscape photographer as the Bath decomposed when agitated in transit. The addition of some carbonate of soda to the Bath, followed by filtering the solution and adding one drop of Glacial acetic acid to every 5 oz of Bath could retard this decomposition.

To sensitize the plate the field photographer had to use his darkroom tent. In the darkroom the photographer rinsed out his Bath trough with water, laid it on some sheets of blotting paper and then poured in the Nitrate Bath. Handling the Nitrate Bath had to be done with care as the solution was corrosive and caused bad staining. He then took the collodion coated plate and rested it collodion-side up on a glass dipper. It was then immersed in the Bath with a slow and steady motion. The cover was placed on the trough. The plate was sensitized in the Bath for varied lengths of time depending upon the weather. In hot temperatures it was immersed for no more than 30-40 seconds. In cold weather 1 to 1$^1/_2$ minutes or even 5 minutes were required. The plate was ready when the liquid flowed in a uniform sheet. Over-immersion caused fogging. Once sensitized, the plate was removed from the Bath and dipper and held vertically upon blotting paper to drain off excess Nitrate Bath. The back was wiped with filtering paper and the plate was placed in clean and dry dark slide ready for carrying to the camera. If the sensitized wet-plate was to be carried a long distance, some 5 or 10 minutes from the darkroom tent, it was folded up in the focusing cloth to avoid light fogging.

It was almost time for exposure. Arriving at the camera site the photographer rested the dark slide with its sensitized wet-plate gently on the ground in a shaded area. He then made the final adjustments to his camera and lens. He made sure that they were free of dust, cobwebs, insects and dew. Removing the lens cap and throwing the focusing cloth over himself and the back of the camera the photographer peered through the ground glass and adjusted his focus, aperture and camera angle taking into account the intensity of the light coming from his image, the limitations of his equipment, the state of the atmosphere and temperature, and the quality of his chemicals and available water. Satisfied that all was in order he inserted the dark slide with its plate into the back of the camera. He then made the exposure.

Exposures for wet-plate collodion landscape photography were relatively long.

Hardwich recommended that with a lens system of 15 inch focus and ³/₈ inch aperture and a collodion of a straw-yellow colour the following exposures were required for best results:

3 minutes for a near view well lighted
30 seconds for a distant view with sky and water
6-10 minutes for interior views
6-10 minutes for forest scenery with light from above.

Ideally, he felt that a good diffused light for three quarters of the exposure time with the sun coming out at the end was preferable, but he assured the photographer that if his chemicals were in good order a long exposure even in the brightest sunlight would give all the correct gradations. [11] It should be noted at this point that photographers in the field occasionally imitated their portrait studio colleagues who deliberately underexposed their plates. These underexposed plates, once processed, were backed with black paper, velvet or paint and this produced a positive image of fine quality and detail. In America these underexposed plates were known as 'ambrotypes' and enjoyed a great measure of popularity during the 1850s, particularly in portrait photography. Whatever exposure was chosen by the landscape photographer, when it was completed the lens cap was replaced and the dark slide removed from the camera. The photographer then either proceeded with further exposures or returned to the darkroom tent to develop the plates.

Development as soon as possible after sensitizing and exposure was advisable in order to avoid dryness and dot formation due to the rapid evaporation of ether and to allow for the free flowing of the developer. The developing agents of the wet-plate era were basically composed of either Pyro-Gallic Acid, Gallic Acid, or Protosalts of Iron used in cold temperatures of 40°F or less. Pyro-Gallic Acid developer was the most common and consisted of a solution of Pyro-Gallic acid (i.e. acid produced by the decomposition and oxidation of tannic acid when powdered gall nuts were exposed for a long time in a moist state to air, producing Gallic Acid, which is heated 410°F to decompose into a white sublimate which then crystalizes), cold water or alcohol or ether, and acetic acid or citric acid (which was best suited for landscapes). Hardwich recommended that Pyrogallic Acid developer be prepared by combining 1 gr. of Pyrogallic Acid, 20 minns. of Glacial Acetic Acid, 1 oz of distilled water, and some silver nitrate if necessary for strengthening the image. He felt that 3 drachms of this developer were needed for a 4″ x 5″ plate, 1 oz for a 9″ x 7″ plate, and 12 drachms for a 10″ x 8″ plate.

Development of the plates was an exacting operation. Once again the photographer confined himself within the darkroom tent. Developing solutions were placed near at hand

11 Hardwich, *op. cit*, p. 267.

with the Pyro-Gallic Acid developer in a small beaker. The exposed plate was removed from the dark slide. If the plate had been out of the sensitizing Nitrate Bath for an extended time the photographer might first decide to redip the plate in the Nitrate Bath before developing. But this was risky as a redipped plate might fog. When it came time to develop, the measured amount of Pyro-Gallic solution was poured evenly on the plate held in the hand. Moving the plate to keep the solution moving backwards and forwards the photographer closely watched the development for 30-40 seconds until the image appeared sufficiently intense. If the image was weak a second portion of developer with some additional silver nitrate was used. Knowing the exact development time was mainly a matter of experience. The development time necessary for a particular plate was dependent upon a number of critical factors including exposure time, the intensity of the original light on the view, and the temperature in the darkroom tent. An under-exposed plate would develop slowly; the highlights would be black, no minor details would be visible. An over-exposed plate would develop quickly, would be a grey or red or brown colour, and the image would be faint and flat. A properly exposed negative would develop normally, having an image partially but not fully seen by reflected light; by transmitted light the image would be bright with a yellow creamy appearance. A view containing a variety of objects which contrast strongly in their power of reflecting light intensity would also determine development time since Pyro-Gallic acid developer could quickly destroy the definition in the light parts in such views. Temperature conditions have a direct effect on development: the hotter the temperature the muddier the acid, the faster the development time, and the greater the possibility of staining; temperatures below 40°F cause the Pyrogallic and acetic acids to work slowly and suppress the dark shades so that the plate appeared underexposed. Satisfied that development was complete the photographer then poured off the excess solution and washed the plate to remove the final traces of developer. The plate could now be brought out of the darkroom tent for further processing. Undoubtedly, the photographer was relieved to get a breath of fresh air after the confines of the tent.

Fixing the negative plate to render the image indestructable by light by removing any unsensitized silver salts could be postponed, but there was a risk that the emulsion would peel. So normally the photographer proceeded with fixing soon after development. There were numerous fixing agents available in the wet-plate era, including alkaline chlorides, iodides and cyanides. Ammonia was used as a fixing agent for paper proofs. But the most common fixer was the universally accepted thiosulphate of soda (Hypo). Hardwich recommended 4 oz of Hypo and 4 oz of common water as an adequate fixer. The photographer poured the Hypo on and off the plate until all the excess iodide was cleared away. The Hypo was then washed away.

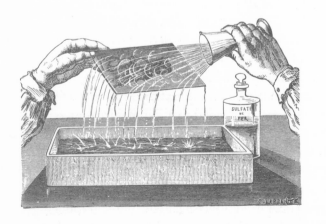

The final washing of the negative plate was best done over a three to four hour period. Laying the plate emulsion-upwards in a dish the photographer bathed it in water, changing the water several times. Once assured that all the Hypo was removed the plate was then placed in the sun or some heated area to dry.

While the plates were being washed or dried the photographer could then begin to dismantle his equipment; carefully repacking his camera, lens and chemicals, and rolling up his darkroom tent. Once the plates were thoroughly dried and he had packed them away, he could then proceed to the next camera site or return from the field.

However, if the photographer had more time available to him or had no need or intention of moving onwards he might varnish the negative plates to protect the emulsion from damage. A varnish that would not crack and yet had sufficient body to protect the emulsion was used. The flask of varnish was placed in hot water for a few minutes and the negative plates were warmed gently before a fire to 140°F or 160°F. The varnish was then filtered through biblous paper and then poured on and off the negative plate. A second coat was never given. The plate was placed aside to dry. Once dry the plates were packed away until the photographer was ready to make positive proofs or prints from them.

Collodion wet-plate landscape photography in the 1850s was an exacting operation requiring definite skills and artistry, a goodly amount of physical stamina and energy, sufficient time, and not a little good fortune in terms of weather, climate and environment. Skills and artistry were learned and perfected with experience and new technological advances. Photographers had to develop sufficient stamina and energy to lug about equipment that weighed up to 120 pounds. Time was governed both by the priorities of the photographer and the restrictions of the photographic system. For the production of a single landscape negative from the time the gear was unpacked until it was repacked at least three and a half hours were required. Five or six hours were probably needed to achieve the best results. Each additional exposure would require an additional ten to fifteen minutes. [12] As for the environment, its climate, weather and geography, no one could control that.

Indeed, the extensive processing time factor, the bulky and cumbersome nature of the photographic system, and the total dependency upon the vagaries of the environment were the three major drawbacks of collodion wet-plate landscape photography. It was the continual striving to reduce bulk and processing time in the field and to make the photographic system less dependent upon the field environment that eventually led to the developments of new techniques and systems. By the 1880s with the commercial availability of gelatin dry-plates and later of roll film the collodion wet-plate photography that had flourished in the 1850s was virtually forgotten.

12 The estimated time span is based on the following compilations: unpack equipment – 5 min; set-up darkroom tent – 1 to 2 min; clean plate – 1 to 2 min; coat with collodion emulsion – 1 min; prepare nitrate Bath – 1/2 min; sensitize plate – 1 to 2 min; remove and blot – 1/5 min; walk to site, set up camera and adjust – 1 to 10 min; expose plate – 1 to 5 min; develop – 1 min; fix – 1/2 min; wash – 2 to 4 hours; dry – 1 to 2 hours; repack – 10 to 15 min; varnish – 1 to 2 hours. Total processing time excluding washing, drying, or varnishing 18 to 40 min. Total processing time including washing and drying: 3 1/4 hours to 6 1/2 hours.

CHAPTER II

Photographic proof and

print making in the 1850s

The collodion wet-plate photographic process of the 1850s, like the earlier Talbotype or Calotype process, was a negative producing system which required a secondary processing stage to create a positive image. These positive images were produced either by directly converting the negative image on the glass plate into a positive or by making separate positive proofs or prints on paper or as glass transparencies.[1]

Direct positives on glass were particularly popular with the portrait photographers although landscape photographers occasionally produced them. Such positives were made from glass-plate negatives which had deliberately been underexposed. These underexposed negatives, once processed, were backed with black paper, velvet or paint. Known in America as ambrotypes, these direct positives on glass rivalled the daguerreotype in quality. They had the advantage of not possessing the mirror reflection characteristics of the daguerreotype. But they also had the daguerreotype's disadvantage of being a unique image, incapable of being reproduced. Indeed, by the end of the 1850s the ambrotype, like the daguerreotype, was rarely produced. The paper print positive and the positive transparency on glass became the accepted photographic images.

Positive transparencies on glass were prepared by methods similar to those used for the making of paper positives. Glass plates were coated with an emulsion of albumen, acetic acid, water, ammonium iodide and ammonium bromide. These coated plates were sensitized in an Aceto-Nitrate Bath. They were then placed in a printing frame in contact with the negative, exposed for several seconds in daylight or 3-4 minutes in gas light, developed in Pyrogallic acid, fixed in Hypo Bath and toned. These positive transparencies on glass were commonly produced for stereoscopic viewing.

The making of paper print positives had been initiated by the Talbotypists and calotypists of the 1840s and perfected by the wet-plate photographers. By the late 1850s there were a number of methods and techniques popularly in use. Three types of photosensitive paper were in general use: albumenized, Ammonio-nitrate, and plain paper. In the preparation of these photosensitive papers photographers required paper stock of the finest quality. English papers were preferred since they were sized with gelatine, retained the photographic salts better, and had a fine smooth texture and surface. French and German papers, on the other hand, were sized with starch, were more porous, and required the addition of gelatine, caseine or albumen to retain the salts at the surface and to provide a smooth surface. The photosensitive paper known as plain paper consisted of paper stock impregnated with a solution of ammonium chloride or sodium chloride, purified gelatine, Iceland Moss and water, and sensitized with silver nitrate and water. Ammonio-Nitrate paper consisted of paper impregnated with a solution of ammonium chloride, gelatine and water and sensitized in a solution of ammonio-nitrate of silver and water. Albumenized

[1] Unless otherwise indicated all facts in this chapter are taken from various sections of T.F. Hardwich's *A Manual of Photographic Chemistry Including the Practice of the Collodion Process* (London: John Churchill, 1859) Fifth Edition.

paper consisted of paper impregnated with a solution of ammonium chloride or pure sodium chloride, water and albumen, and sensitized in a solution of silver nitrate and water. Albumenized paper was the simplest to process and generally useful. Ammonio-Nitrate paper required greater expertise in handling but gave excellent results when black tones were desired. Plain paper was easier to manipulate than Ammonio-Nitrate and was better adapted for toning by the Sel d'or bath than Albumenized paper. These photosensitive papers were either purchased commercially from the photographic establishments or produced by the photographer.

Paper positive proofs and prints using these photosensitive papers could be made by two methods known at the time as 'the direct action by light' process and 'the negative printing process upon chloride of silver'. The former was the easiest and preferred method while the latter was much more difficult and required the skill of 'a perfect master of the art'.

The direct action by light process required a number of simple manipulations which, if carried through correctly, would normally produce good proofs or prints. A printing frame consisting of a wooden box-like structure with a glass front and a wooden back or shutter was the only piece of specialized equipment needed. Working in the daylight or in a darkroom if the outside light was too strong the photographer first removed the shutter from the frame. The negative was then laid flat upon the frame glass and the photo paper placed upon the negative sensitized side downwards. A layer of thick felt followed and the whole was tightly compressed by replacing and bolting down the shutter. The negative and paper were then exposed to the sunlight.

The length of exposure necessary to produce a proper image on the paper by this method varied with the density of the negative and the intensity of the light rays as influenced by the season of the year and the prevailing weather conditions. 10-15 minutes were necessary when the light was strong in the early spring or summer. But in the winter $^3/_4$ to $1^1/_2$ hours even in the direct rays of the sun were required. Hardwich reports that in a dull London light some four days might be spent to get one impression. The photographer would have to judge for himself when the print was ready. This he did by examining the tonal changes of the paper. The examination was either done inside or in the open air if the photographer was careful and worked speedily. According to Hardwich

If the general aspect of the print is a rich chocolate brown in the case of Albumen, a dark slate-blue with Ammonio-Nitrate paper, or a reddish purple with paper prepared with chloride and Citrate of Silver, or Chloride and Serum of Milk, probably the subsequent parts of the process will proceed well.

When the paper appeared ready, the photographer removed it from the frame. He now had a positive paper proof with an image which would last for some hours if kept in a dark place but would fade upon continued exposure to light. For a permanent and finished print the photographer had to fix and tone the proof.

To fix the image the proof was immersed in a Hypo Bath and moved about to displace air bubbles. Normally there was no prior washing of the proof as the photographers felt they needed the free silver nitrate to aid in the toning. Immediately upon coming into contact with the Hypo Bath the chocolate brown or violet tint of the image disappeared and left the image with a red tone: Albumen proofs became brick red while Ammonio-Nitrate proofs became sepia or brown-black. After the proof had been thoroughly reddened the final toning action began.

The toning action on the image in the Hypo Bath was continued until the desired effect was obtained. With a Hypo solution in good working order and a temperature at 60°F, toning might have been completed in 10-15 minutes. The brown and purple tones of the image were the earlier stages of colouration; then the black tones which took more time. The ultimate colour of the print varied with the density of the negative, the character of the subject, and the length of immersion in the Hypo Bath. Prolonged immersion was avoided as it led to sulphuration, yellowness, and eventual fading in the half-tones of the print. Aside from immersion in the Hypo Bath there were other contemporary methods of toning which were more troublesome but gave better uniformity of colour and greater permanency. One method was the Sel d'Or process used for Plain paper. It consisted of a solution of gold chloride, pure Hypo, Hydrochloric acid and water. The other method was known as the Alkaline Chloride of Gold process. This was used for toning Albumenized paper. It consisted of a solution of gold chloride, sesquicarbonate of soda, citric acid and water.

Once toned and fixed the print was removed from the bath and all traces of Hypo and toner washed out with water. The slow running of cold water over the print in a large shallow vessel for 4-5 hours was recommended, but if running water were not available the prints were to be placed in trays with water which was changed 5-6 times every fifteen minutes for the 4-5 hours. Dabbing the prints with a sponge greatly reduced the washing time. Finally the prints were removed from the wash, immersed in boiling water to remove the sizing and ensure permanency, blotted, and then hung to dry. The making of positive prints by the direct action of light process was now completed.

The second method of obtaining positive proofs or prints was the difficult Negative Printing Process upon Chloride of Silver. It was most useful during the winter months when the light was feeble. It was also the method used when it was necessary to produce a large number of prints from a negative within a short time. Basically the method involved exposing paper prepared with silver chloride to light for a brief time until a faint image was perceptible and then developing the image with Gallic Acid. Paper stock was impregnated with a solution of ammonium chloride, citric acid, sesquicarbonate of soda, gelatine and distilled water. Afterward, it was sensitized in a solution of silver nitrate, glacial acetic acid and water, and left to dry. The paper was then placed in the printing frame with the negative and exposed to either bright or dull light for 3-4 minutes until a faint image appeared. On removal from the frame, the paper was developed for 3-6 minutes in a solution of Gallic acid and water. The print was washed, fixed and gold toned in the same way as the prints prepared by the direct action of light process.

Positive prints prepared by either method had virtually the same stability and appearance. A well prepared print had rich tones of brown or black, was warm and bright in appearance with good definition and contrast, and was free from spots, stains, streaks, or yellowness. Generally positives printed on English papers assumed some shade of brown more or less removed from black whereas the darker tones were more readily obtained upon foreign papers. However, prints of uniform tint were hard to achieve consistently because manufacturers of the paper used different sizing in their processes.

The dimensions of most paper positive proofs and prints of the 1850s were dependent upon the size of the negative since they were contacts produced directly in conjunction with the negative. Systems for enlarging or reducing images were known but these were not to come into general use until the 1860s. Thus, paper positives invariably approximated in size the standard negative sizes – $2^1/_2''$ x $2''$, $3^1/_4''$ x $2^3/_4''$, $4^1/_4''$ x $3^1/_4''$, $5''$ x $4''$, $6^1/_2''$ x $4^3/_4''$, $8^1/_2''$ x $6^1/_2''$, $10''$ x $8''$ and $12''$ x $10''$. Trimming was at the discretion of the individual photographer. It was a common practice to round the corners, particularly of landscape views where the lens limitations of astigmatism and field curvature were obvious.

Unmounted prints were stored loosely or sometimes placed in albums or scrapbooks with slits cut in the pages to insert the corners of the prints. Prints could be mounted on mattes or in albums by using a variety or adhesives either prepared commercially or at home. However, a solution of gelatine ('Scotch Glue') in hot water or some caoutchouc dissolved in mineral naptha was the recommended mounting adhesive.

The survival today of excellent paper prints from the 1850s is attributable in part to the quality of the paper stock. The preferred papers were generally of rag and free from sulphurs, chlorides and other bleaches and acids which in time not only destroy the paper but react harmfully with the photographic emulsion. The survival of such prints is also attributable to the diligence, care, skill and knowledge of the photographers and to the toning processes they employed. The making of a photographic image in the 1850s was a costly, physically demanding, and time-consuming operation from the initial negative making to the final processing of the print. Most photographers would exercise a great deal of caution to ensure that the final outcome of their work, the positive image, was of the best possible quality. They were well aware that fading and deterioration of prints was as often due to their own mistakes as to the imperfect nature of their photo materials and the environment about them. Hardwich pointed out a host of possible causes for fading and deterioration of prints: imperfect washing and fixing, oxidation and sulphuration occasioned by processing, improper mounting, decomposition of pyroxyline inherent in the collodion, and impurities in the air from sewers, drains and coal gas. He cautioned photographers to be careful in their processing and recommended simple steps to prevent fading and guarantee permanence. He correctly stated that the best guarantees of permanence were in the gold toning processes. For indeed, in the effort to obtain a deep richness of tone the photographers of the 1850s, either wittingly or unwittingly, also assured their photographic images of a longevity well beyond their wildest expectations. Gold toning to this day remains the best means to achieve photographic permanence.

Bibliography and

notes on the illustrations

Unpublished Sources

Church of St Stephen-in-the-Fields, Toronto. *Baptisms, Marriages, Burials Register* 1858-1871, 1861-1884.

Manitoba Archives, Winnipeg. Hind, Henry Youle Collection, Assiniboine and Saskatchewan Exploring
   Expedition; Note Book No. 5 Kept by H.L. Hime, July 20–27, 1858 ...
– St. Andrews Parish Register 1860–1883, No. 315.

– Morton, W.L. Manuscript biography of Henry Youle Hind.

Public Archives of Canada, Provincial Secretary's Office Canada West, Record Group 5, C I Volumes 578–579,
   1858 Red River Exploration No. 1718; Volume 707; Volume 918 No. 1501 File 1718; Correspondence
   Registry 1862 No. 557 and Analytical Index.
– Records of the Executive Council, Record Group 1, State Book S.
– Indian Affairs Branch, Record Group 10, Volume 221, Indian Affairs Register 1852–56, No. 8904.
– Department of Finance, Record Group 19, d2 (d), Volume 1931–1932; Volume 2611 Copies of Orders in
   Council 10 Sept. 1858.
– Statistics Canada Census Records, 1825–1871, 1871 Toronto, St Patrick's Ward C Division No. 2. Reel
   C-633.
– Church Missionary Society Records, Manuscript Group 17 C 1./o A-84 Henry Budd Journal; A-92-93 Rev
   A. Cowley Journal and William W. Kirkby Jrnl.
– Fur Trade and Indians, E, Red River Settlement, Manuscript Group 19; A-28 Samuel Taylor Diary; E-7
   John Inkster Volumes 1–5; D-14 Fort Ellice Journal Entries; Dr Wm. Cowan E-8 Volumes 1–2.
– Post-Confederation Manuscripts, Manuscript Group 29, F 66 Sgt. John Balmer autobiography.

Surrogate Court of the County of York, Toronto, Ontario. Index County of York 1887–1910, Grant No. 16525,
   Probate Grant. Register Book Folio 400, Last Will and Testament H.L. Hime Oct. 17, 1903, Inventory H.L.
   Hime estate, December 1903.

Published Sources

Adam, G. Mercer. *Toronto, Old and New: A Memorial Volume: Historical, Descriptive and Pictorial*. Toronto: The
   Mail Printing Company, 1891.

Anon. *Brown's Toronto General Directory* 1861-62.
– *Canada Directory* 1857-1858.
– *Canada Directory* 1870.
– *Mitchell's Canada Business Directory* 1864-65.
– *Narrative of The Canadian Red River Exploring Expedition ... Opinions of the Press*. Toronto: Maclean and Co, c.
   1861.

Boni, A. *Photographic Literature*. Hastings-on-Hudson, 1963.

Boon, T.C.B. *The Anglican Church from the Bay to the Rockies: A History of the Ecclesiastical Province of Rupert's Land and its Diocese from* 1820-1950. Toronto: Ryerson Press, c. 1962.

Canada: Legislative Assembly. *Report on the Exploration of the Country Between Lake Superior and the Red River Settlement*. Toronto: J. Lovell, 1858.
– *Sessional Papers, Canada* 1858. Report of the Auditor. Appendix No. 12. Toronto, 1859.
– *North-West Territory, Reports of Progress; Together With A Preliminary And General Report On The Assiniboine and Saskatchewan Exploring Expedition, Made Under Instructions From The Provincial Secretary, Canada* (by Henry Youle Hind). Toronto: J. Lovell, 1859.

Canadian Journal of Science, Literature and History. Series 2, Volumes V and VI, 1860–61.

Daily Leader. Toronto: July 31, 1877.

Gernshein, Helmut and Alison. *The History of Photography from the Earliest Use of the Camera Obscura in the Eleventh Century up to 1914*. Toronto: Oxford University Press, 1955.

Globe. Toronto, 1858, 1873, and 1903.

Greenhill, R. *Early Photography in Canada*. Toronto: Oxford University Press, 1965.
– 'Early Canadian Photographer, Humphrey Lloyd Hime', *Image*, The Bulletin of The George Eastman House of Photography, Vol. II, No. 3, 1962, pps. 9–11.

Hardwich, Thomas Frederick. *A Manual of Photographic Chemistry including the Practice of the Collodion Process*. First Edition, London: 1855. Fifth Edition, London: John Churchill, 1859.
– *Manual of Photographic Chemistry*. New York: Humphrey, First Edition 1855, Second Edition 1856, Fourth Edition, 1858.

Hind, H.Y. *Narrative of the Canadian Red River Exploring Expedition of* 1857 *and of the Assiniboine and Saskatchewan Exploring Expedition of* 1858. Volumes I and II. London: Longman, Green, Longman and Roberts, 1860.

Illustrated London News. London: Volume XXXIII; No. 939, October 2, 1858; No. 941, October 16, 1858.

Ingram, G.C. 'Industrial and Agricultural Activities at Lower Fort Garry'. Occasional Papers in Archaeology and History. No. 4. Ottawa: Information Canada-Canadian Historic Sites, 1971.

Journal of the Synod of the Church of England in the Diocese of Toronto, 1872. Toronto: 1873.

Mail. Toronto: November, 1903.

Masters, D.C. *The Rise of Toronto* 1850-1890. Toronto: University of Toronto Press, 1947.

Morton, W.L. *Manitoba: A History*. Toronto: University of Toronto Press, 1957.

Pollack, P. *The Picture History of Photography*. New York: Harry N. Abrams, 1969.

Rudisill, R. *Mirror Image*. Albuquerque: University of New Mexico Press, 1971.

Snider, C.H.J. *Annuals of the Royal Canadian Yacht Club* 1852–1937. Toronto: 1937.

Sutton, T. *Photographic Notes*. Volume 6, No. 114, London, January 1, 1861.

Taft, R. *Photography and the American Scene: A Social History*, 1831-1889. New York: Dover Publications, 1964.

Thomas, D.B. *Science Museum Photography Collection*. London: Her Majesty's Stationary Office, 1969.

Toronto City Council. *Minutes of the Council* 1873–74. .

Transactions of the Board of Agriculture and of the Agricultural Association of Upper Canada. Toronto: Thompson; Volume 2, 1858, Volume 5, 1860.

United Kingdom. *Report of Progress Together with a Preliminary and General Report, on the Assiniboine and Saskatch-ewan Exploring Expedition*, by H.Y. Hind. London: Her Majesty's Printing Office, 1860.

Warkentin, J. *The Western Interior of Canada: A Record of Geographical Discovery* 1612-1917. Toronto: Carleton Library No. 15, McClelland and Stewart, 1964.

Notes on the illustrations

Part One. The Portfolio plates numbered 3 to 49 were made from original H. L. Hime prints in the collections of the Public Archives of Canada. Portfolio plate no. 1 was made from the original H. L. Hime print in the Baldwin Room of the Toronto Public Library. Portfolio plate no. 2 was reproduced from an engraving in the *Illustrated London News*, Volume XXXIII, October, 1858, held by the National Library of Canada.

Part Two. The small side plates are from H. L. Hime prints in the collection of the Public Archives of Canada. The sources of the remaining illustrations are as follows:

Public Archives of Canada, Record Group 5, C 1, Vol. 707, No. 557. Invoice of the Firm Armstrong, Beere and Hime, May 4, 1859.

H. L. Hime print in the Hind Album, Baldwin Room, Toronto Public Library

Illustrated London News, Vol. XXXIII, October, 1858.

Illustrated London News, Vol. XXXIII, October, 1858.

Public Archives of Canada, National Photography Collection Accession No. 1970-88. Embossed seal of Armstrong, Beere and Hime affixed to photograph mount.

Public Archives of Canada, National Photography Collection Accession No. 1970-88. Signature of H. L. Hime on photograph entitled 'Tents on the prairie'.

Part Three. The illustrations are reproduced from Tissandier, Gaston, *A History and Handbook of Photography*. Second edition. London: Sampson Low, Marston, Searle & Rivington, 1878. Reprinted in The Literature of Photography Series by Arno Press, New York, 1973.

The Maps. The map facing page 5 and the map on page 20 are reproduced from Hind, H. Y., *Narrative of the Canadian Red River Exploring Expedition of 1857 and of the Assiniboine and Saskatchewan Exploring Expedition of 1858*. Volume I. London, 1860.

This book has been printed in an edition of 2000 copies,
Fall 1975, by The Coach House Press, Toronto.
The papers are Carlyle Japan Plate and Rolland Zephyr book laid.
The type is Janson.
The plates are micrograin duotone photo offset reproductions from the original photographic prints.
Published with the kind assistance of the Canada Council and the Ontario Arts Council.